C0-GIM-611

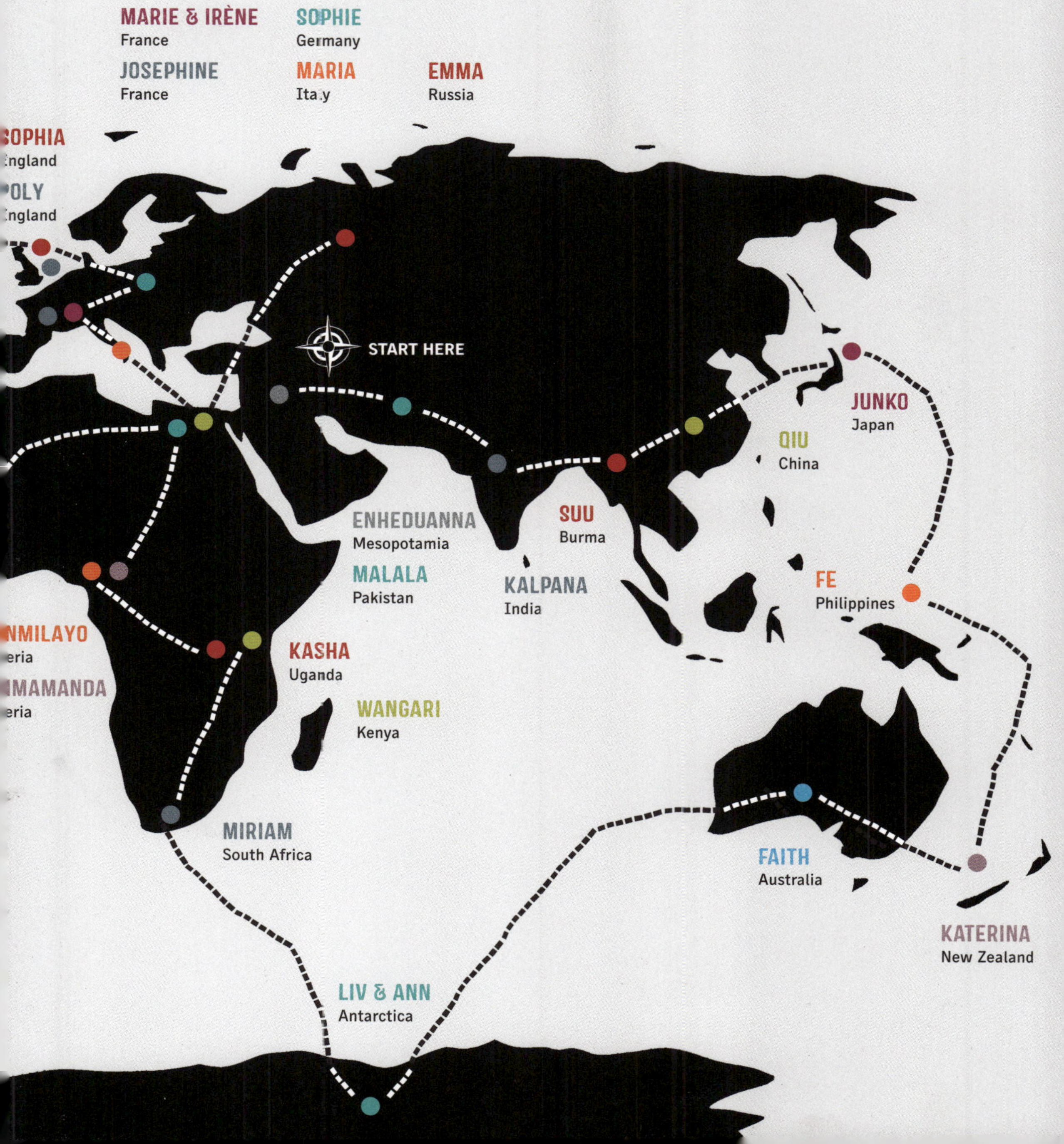
MARIE & IRÈNE
France
SOPHIE
Germany
JOSEPHINE
France
MARIA
Italy
EMMA
Russia
OPHIA
ngland
OLY
ngland
START HERE
JUNKO
Japan
QIU
China
ENHEDUANNA
Mesopotamia
SUU
Burma
MALALA
Pakistan
KALPANA
India
FE
Philippines
NMILAYO
eria
MAMANDA
eria
KASHA
Uganda
WANGARI
Kenya
MIRIAM
South Africa
FAITH
Australia
KATERINA
New Zealand
LIV & ANN
Antarctica

RAD WOMEN WORLDWIDE

MIRIAM MAKEBA

RAD WOMEN WORLDWIDE

ARTISTS AND ATHLETES, PIRATES AND PUNKS, AND OTHER REVOLUTIONARIES WHO SHAPED HISTORY

WRITTEN BY
KATE SCHATZ

ILLUSTRATED BY
MIRIAM KLEIN STAHL

HAYS PUBLIC LIBRARY

TEN SPEED PRESS
BERKELEY

Text copyright © 2016 by Kate Schatz
Illustrations copyright © 2016 by Miriam Klein Stahl

All rights reserved.
Published in the United States by Ten Speed Press,
an imprint of the Crown Publishing Group,
a division of Penguin Random House LLC, New York.
www.crownpublishing.com
www.tenspeed.com

Ten Speed Press and the Ten Speed Press
colophon are registered trademarks
of Penguin Random House LLC.

Library of Congress Cataloging-in-Publication
Data is on file with the Publisher.

Hardcover ISBN: 978-0-399-57886-1
eBook ISBN: 978-0-399-57887-8

Printed in China

Design by Angelina Cheney

Running text font, Skopex Gothic,
designed by Andrea Tinnes

10 9 8 7 6 5 4 3 2 1

First Edition

For Benson and Ivy, and Hazel, once again

For Great-Aunt Doris, for Nana,
and for our mothers

CONTENTS

"DON'T TELL ME WOMEN AREN'T THE STUFF OF HEROES."
—QIU JIN

FRIDA KAHLO &
CHAVELA VARGAS

WELCOME TO *RAD WOMEN WORLDWIDE!*

Close your eyes and picture a pirate. Now picture a spy. Imagine a president. A warrior in battle. A great painter. A computer programmer. A doctor. A soccer player. A pharaoh.

The women in this book are all these things, and more.

Imagine Antarctica. Do you see two strong women trudging across the ice, about to set a world record? How about ancient Egypt: can you picture a female king ordering the construction of a massive temple? Visualize the snowy peak of Mt. Everest, and the climber who's just reached the top: her name is Junko Tabei. In Nigeria, a best-selling author is writing her next book. On a big green soccer field, during the World Cup, a goal was just scored. Can you picture the bouncing ponytail of Marta, one of the greatest players of all time?

Welcome to *Rad Women Worldwide*. Think of this book as a journey around the world: the 40 stories take place on every continent, and span millennia. They tell about the lives and accomplishments of bold, brave women who lived awesome, exciting, revolutionary, historic, and world-changing lives—in other words, they're *rad*. Some lived thousands of years ago; others are alive today. Some are known all over the world for their achievements, some are revered in just their home countries, and some still await the recognition they deserve. No matter what country or century they're from, these women are passionate, purposeful, and totally powerful. In the face of doubt and danger, they defied tradition, broke rules, and kept going. They spoke up, they sang, they wrote, they fought.

The history of the world is vast, amazing, and fascinating. But so often the stories we hear and lessons we learn focus on the contributions and actions of men. In this book you'll learn about women and events you might never have heard of, and places you might never have been. Learning about what has happened beyond our own borders increases our understanding of the whole world, and it can help us learn more about ourselves, too.

Together, these stories show the immense range of what women have done and can do. Of course, this book is just one small step in a miles-long journey through the history of rad women. For every story you read, there are hundreds (thousands!) more to be told.

We hope that all readers—girls and boys, teachers and parents, young and old—will find inspiration, encouragement, and worldwide wonder in these stories.

May we all have the courage to be rad. Now, let's get started!

ENHEDUANNA

2285 – 2250 BCE (UR, MESOPOTAMIA)

"MY KING, SOMETHING HAS BEEN CREATED THAT NO ONE HAS CREATED BEFORE."

Enheduanna, who lived 4,300 years ago, is the world's oldest known author. Yes, before the ancient Greek poet Sappho, before Confucius, even before *The Epic of Gilgamesh*, there was Enheduanna: a priestess, princess, poet, and teacher who lived, wrote, and ruled as part of the world's most ancient society. Her story is also the story of the beginning of the written word—and of civilization as we know it!

At this time, the countries of Iraq, Syria, and Turkey were part of an ancient region called Mesopotamia, where many believe that civilization began. It's also where the first form of writing was developed. Cuneiform script, a system of wedge-shaped marks carved into clay tablets, was used for 3,000 years as the script for a number of languages. The clay tablets have lasted thousands of years and are the very first pieces of writing ever discovered. Many tablets contain written laws, prayers, and business letters.

In 1927, in the desert sands of Iraq, a fragment of one of these clay tablets was discovered. It included images of a woman, and was inscribed with the name "Enheduanna." Archeologists soon found 100 more fragments covered with hymns, poems, songs, and stories, all attributed to the same writer.

Since their discovery and excavation, at least three of Enheduanna's major works have been translated into English from the ancient Sumerian language: two are hymns of devotion to Inanna, the powerful goddess of love, war, and fertility. "The Exaltation of Inanna" is 153 lines long, and it is filled with love and admiration for the great goddess. It also tells the story of how Enheduanna was forced by her enemies to leave her throne; she thanks Inanna for helping her return and reclaim her position of power.

We now know that Enheduanna was born to the powerful King Sargon of Akkad and his wife, Queen Tashlultum. King Sargon is considered by some to be the first emperor, and he unified Central and South Mesopotamia. He appointed his daughter as High Priestess, a role of major political, spiritual, and social importance; she's the first known woman to have held this title.

Enheduanna's writing is remarkable not just for how old it is but also for how good it is, and how personal. Her hymns and poems express her passionate emotions, from joy and love to fear and anger. She also wrote in first person, meaning she used "I" and "me" instead of "she" and "he." Her voice is confident and strong. Her writing tells us that she traveled extensively, as she describes in detail the beauty of a number of temples. Her writings were copied and honored for centuries and are believed to have had great influence on the development of literature and religion for the next 1,000 years.

MALALA YOUSAFZAI

JULY 12, 1997 (MINGORA, PAKISTAN)

"WHEN THE WHOLE WORLD IS SILENT, EVEN ONE VOICE BECOMES POWERFUL."

Malala Yousafzai was in chemistry class when a teacher came into the room with exciting news. "Malala! You've won the Nobel Peace Prize!" At 17, Malala was the youngest person—and the first Pakistani—to win the prestigious award. Her classmates cheered, and Malala hugged her teacher. Then she went back to her studies and finished the school day.

Just three years earlier, Malala had lain in a hospital bed in Pakistan, fighting for her life. The 14-year-old had been shot in the head, and no one expected her to survive. If she did make it, her doctors said, she almost certainly wouldn't be able to walk, read, or speak.

The men who shot Malala were part of a terrorist group called the Taliban, who believe women and girls should not have rights. They controlled her town in northwest Pakistan, near the Afghanistan border. They banned television, destroyed schools, and attacked girls who tried to learn.

When Malala was 11, a British news organization called the BBC had wanted to find a local schoolgirl to write about what it was like to live under extremist rule. They reached out to Malala's father, a teacher, and asked if his daughter would like to do it. He knew it would be dangerous, but Malala overheard his conversation and insisted that she do it. "Why not me?" she asked. She wanted to speak up for herself, and for the girls in her community.

Malala's diary was published on the BBC's website for 10 weeks, and people all over the world read her story. The first entry described a bad dream she'd had: "I had a terrible dream yesterday with military helicopters and the Taliban. I have had such dreams since the launch of the military operation in Swat. My mother made me breakfast and I went off to school. I was afraid . . ."

This brought Malala respect and admiration, but it also made her a target. Even though the diary was published under a pretend name ("Gul Makai," the heroine of a Pashtun folktale), Malala's identity was eventually discovered. Here was a 14-year-old girl who would not be silenced, and this made grown men terrified. The Taliban sent an assassin to find and kill her. A gunman found her on a schoolbus. He did manage to shoot her, but he didn't manage to take her life or her spirit. In fact, it only made her stronger.

Malala's recovery was miraculous and fast. The world was outraged by the attack, and the publicity Malala received gave her a platform to speak about what is most important to her: peace and education. She wrote a best-selling book, *I Am Malala*, and has traveled around the world, meeting everyone from Queen Elizabeth to Madonna.

CONTINUED

Some call her "The Bravest Girl in the World," and not just because she survived the attack. When she met President Obama, she directly challenged America's use of drone strikes that kill innocent people in Pakistan. She urges world leaders to invest in "books, not bombs," and her organization, the Malala Fund, is opening schools around the world. In her Nobel Prize acceptance speech, she dedicated the award to all the girls who cannot attend school. She's also committed to her own education: she passed her final exams with all As, and plans to attend university.

Like many children around the world, Malala was born into a place of great turmoil. But her region of the world is also rich with history, traditions, and strong female leaders. In fact, Malala is named after Malalai of Maiwand, a famous Afghan heroine. During a war in 1880, a female teenager named Malalai shouted words of inspiration to the Afghan soldiers who were losing to the British. Malalai was shot down by the enemy, but her actions motivated the soldiers, and they won the battle. Malalai became a national hero, and now Malala is fulfilling the destiny of her namesake. Unlike Malalai, Malala survived the bullet, and has gone on to inspire others. A survivor of violence and hatred, Malala fights with a truly powerful weapon: her voice.

KALPANA CHAWLA

MARCH 17, 1962 (KARNAL, INDIA) – FEBRUARY 1, 2003 (TEXAS, U.S.A.)

"THE PATH FROM DREAMS TO SUCCESS DOES EXIST. MAY YOU HAVE THE VISION TO FIND IT, THE COURAGE TO GET ONTO IT."

—MESSAGE SENT TO STUDENTS FROM SPACE

When Kalpana Chawla's math professor explained the concept of a "null set," she used the example of a female Indian astronaut. There had never been one, so it was a classic case of a category that simply did not exist. "Who knows?" Kalpana exclaimed to her class. "One day this set may exist!" The other students laughed—they had no idea that their outspoken classmate would one day make history.

The name *Kalpana* means "imagination." It's perfect for a curious girl who loved the sky. As a child Kalpana would sit on the roof with her brother, watching planes soar overhead. She made elaborate school projects depicting twinkling stars and the universe. Their small town in northern India had a flying club, and Kalpana often convinced her father to take her for rides in small planes and gliders. Soon Kalpana became fascinated with more than the sky—she wanted to know about space.

She was a strong student in math and science. Her teachers encouraged her to continue her education, and she went to college to become an aeronautical engineer. That wasn't common for most girls in her town, who usually got married and became housewives.

In college Kalpana was the only woman in most of her classes, and counselors often urged her to choose a different career. But she persisted, got her PhD, and moved to America to work as a researcher for NASA. Kalpana was selected out of 2,000 applicants for the U.S. astronaut program, and in 1997 her dreams came true: she and five other astronauts traveled 252 times around the earth, or 6.5 million miles.

From space she gazed down at the earth, which she described as looking "sacred." She saw India, the deep green Ganges River, the golden brown Sahara Desert. Her favorite memory was watching the sun rise and set. "It is almost as if everything is in fast forward. Totally dark to violet, to orange and red . . . and then it's sunrise. At the sunset, there was a moon—its crescent was razor sharp, and the color was dusty silvery. Then the moon raced away from us and was lost in the glow of the earth's curvature. Almost like a storybook that you read as a child."

In 2003, Kalpana was thrilled to return to space on the STS-107 *Colombia* mission. She helped conduct nearly 80 microgravity experiments and was the primary operator of the shuttle's robotic arm. After two weeks in space, when the shuttle reentered the earth's atmosphere, tragedy occurred: with a wing damaged during the launch, the space shuttle broke apart. Kalpana and her fellow astronauts did not survive. As the first Indian-born woman to travel to space, Kalpana has become a hero to people all over the world, especially girls who now know that "an Indian woman astronaut" is no longer a "null set."

AUNG SAN SUU KYI

JUNE 19, 1945 (YANGON, BURMA)

"YOU SHOULD NEVER LET YOUR FEARS PREVENT YOU FROM DOING WHAT YOU KNOW IS RIGHT."

When Aung San Suu Kyi traveled to her home country of Burma in 1988, she expected to stay for a few weeks, then return to her husband and two sons in England. She didn't intend to become the leader of her country, a Nobel Peace Prize winner, or an international symbol of the struggle for democracy.

Aung San Suu Kyi ("Aung San" from her father, "Suu" from her grandmother, and "Kyi" from her mother) was born and raised in Burma (also known as Myanmar). Her father, General Aung San, helped negotiate Burma's independence from Britain. He was assassinated when Suu was only two, and he became a national hero. From an early age, Suu believed it was her destiny to someday finish the work her father started.

Suu left Burma as a teenager to study in India, the United States, and England, where she met her husband, Michael. They started a family in London, but Suu made one thing very clear: if there were ever a reason for her to go back to help her beloved country, she would do it.

In 1988, Suu went to Burma to care for her sick mother. The country was in chaos. Ever since Suu's father's death, Burma had been ruled by an oppressive military government. The ruling general had just stepped down, and students, workers, and even monks were taking to the streets to demand change. The police cracked down hard and hurt the protestors. Suu saw the need for leadership, and on August 26, 1988, she gave a speech to half a million people. People came from all over to listen to the hero's daughter as she called for a democratic government. She told them, "I could not, as my father's daughter, remain indifferent to all that was going on."

Suu's moment had come. She helped start a new political party, and she traveled the country holding pro-democracy rallies. In 1989, one year after her return, Suu was arrested and imprisoned in her own home. Armed guards were present day and night, and no visitors were allowed—including her own family. She remained there for the next 15 years, unable to see her sons or her husband—even when he was dying of cancer.

Suu spent these years meditating, studying Buddhism, sewing, exercising—and refusing to give up. When she was allowed to walk to the walls around her house, she would climb up to the top and give speeches to crowds of people, never ceasing in her call for peace and democracy.

Suu was finally released for good in 2010. In 2015 Burma held elections, and Suu's party won almost 80 percent of Parliament seats. Suu herself won a parliamentary seat, ending almost 50 years of military rule. It will take time before change will happen throughout Burma, but there is hope that justice will prevail—thanks to the tireless efforts of Aung San Suu Kyi.

QIU JIN

NOVEMBER 8, 1875 (XIAMEN, CHINA) – JULY 15, 1907 (SHAOXING, CHINA)

"WITH ALL MY HEART I BESEECH AND BEG MY 200 MILLION FEMALE COMPATRIOTS TO ASSUME THEIR RESPONSIBILITY AS CITIZENS. ARISE! ARISE! CHINESE WOMEN, ARISE!"

The "modern-day Mulan." The "Chinese Joan of Arc." "China's first feminist." These names have all been used to describe Qiu Jin, who defied tradition to become a revolutionary leader in China's Qing dynasty.

Qiu Jin was born in the Fujian Province of southeastern China. Her early life was traditional: she went to school, loved horses and books, and did as she was told. Following traditional practice, her feet were wrapped tightly in cloth to prevent them from developing properly. Small feet were considered more beautiful, but it was a painful and debilitating practice. When she was 21, in 1896, her father forced her to get married.

China was then undergoing a major transition. After nearly 300 years under the rule of the corrupt Qing dynasty, many believed it was time for change. Revolution was in the air—and so were new ideas about women's roles in society. During a trip to Beijing, Qiu heard all about this. She wanted to know more, so she studied feminist literature. She couldn't stand her husband, writing that he treated her as "less than nothing." These developments gave her the courage to do something unheard of: she left her marriage, sold her jewelry to raise money, and moved by herself to Tokyo, Japan.

There Qiu joined several secret societies committed to overthrowing the Chinese government. She believed change could not occur until men and women were equal. She admired Hua Mulan, the Chinese warrior who had dressed like a man in order to take her father's place in the army. Qiu also studied martial arts, and wearing men's suits became her trademark. She often carried a sword, calling herself "Jin Xiong," or "able to compete with men."

Qiu wanted to share her ideas with as many women as possible. She wrote essays, but many Chinese women couldn't read, so she gave energetic speeches about women's rights. She also wrote beautiful poetry, with lines like "Unbinding my feet I clean out a thousand years of poison / With heated heart arouse all women's spirits."

Returning to China in 1906, she started a feminist magazine that encouraged women to pursue education, find jobs, and become financially independent. Qiu also worked with a close comrade to unify radical activist groups. In 1907, while teaching at a school that was a secret training ground for revolutionary soldiers, she learned that her comrade had been caught. She knew she'd be next. Qiu Jin was arrested and charged with the crime of writing two revolutionary poems. Her execution shocked the nation and made her a hero to many and a symbol of women's independence. Four years after her death, the Revolution of 1911 transformed China, bringing about the change she had fought for.

JUNKO TABEI

SEPTEMBER 22, 1939 (MIHARU, JAPAN)

"THERE WAS NEVER A QUESTION IN MY MIND THAT I WANTED TO CLIMB THAT MOUNTAIN, NO MATTER WHAT OTHER PEOPLE SAID."

It was the morning of May 16, 1975, and 35-year-old Junko Tabei, a Japanese housewife and mother, dug her spiked boots into the ice and crawled across a slick, narrow ridge. Just four foot nine, Junko was standing almost 30,000 feet above sea level, and her destination was only 40 feet away: the South Summit of Mt. Everest, the tallest mountain in the world. On that freezing morning, Junko became the first woman to ever reach it.

Junko was born in a small town in northern Japan. She fell in love with climbing at 10 years old on a school field trip. She and her classmates hiked up two tall peaks, Mount Asahi and Mount Chausu. She longed to climb more, but her family was poor, and mountain climbing wasn't something they could afford. It also wasn't seen as an activity for girls, especially small ones. When she went off to college, she joined several climbing clubs, where she was almost always the only woman. After she graduated, she founded the Ladies Climbing Club of Japan and began to scale peaks with other female climbers.

In 1975 Junko and 14 other women planned the first all-woman Everest expedition, with Junko as leader. The women and their sherpas (Himalayan people who assist climbers) completed a long and rigorous training process before embarking on their record-setting journey. Junko's husband and three-year-old daughter cheered for her as she set off to climb to the top of the world, but many people were shocked that a mother would leave her family behind to do anything, let alone climb a mountain! "We were told we should be raising children instead," Junko said.

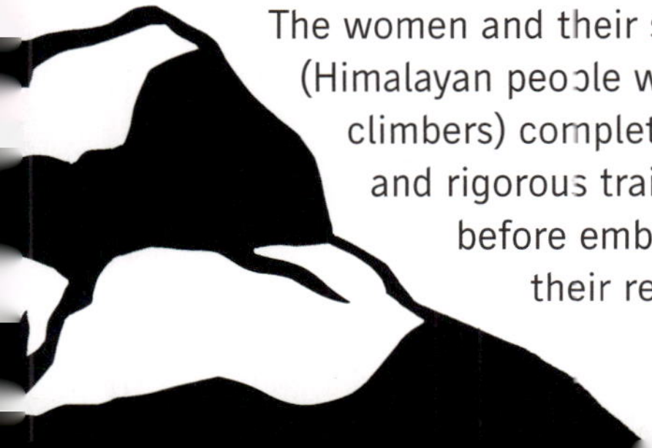

But Junko was determined, and her family's support was all she needed. The women set off, well-prepared and excited, but the journey was dangerous. One cold morning on the mountain, Junko woke up to a thunderous sound: an avalanche. Soon a massive wave of snow, rocks, and ice had buried Junko and several others. Junko was unconscious for six full minutes. Her fellow climbers pulled her out of the snow and revived her with an oxygen mask. She was bruised and battered, but she continued on.

When she finally reached the top, Junko peered down thousands of feet into the valleys of Tibet. She was exhausted and relieved to have made it. She was also very proud. Junko made history when she reached the top of Everest, but she didn't stop there. In 1992 she became the first woman to climb the "Seven Summits," the highest mountains on each of the seven continents, including Mt. Kilimanjaro in Africa and Mt. Aconcagua in South America. Junko is in her 70s now, but she still climbs at least three or four mountains each year, and has no plans to stop.

FE DEL MUNDO

NOVEMBER 27, 1911 – AUGUST 6, 2011 (MANILA, PHILIPPINES)

"I FEEL THAT IF YOU GIVE THE WORLD THE BEST THAT YOU CAN, THE BEST WILL COME BACK TO YOU."

Fe del Mundo arrived at Harvard Medical School in Boston, Massachusetts, at age 24, in 1936. The journey from her home in Manila, the Philippines' capital, had been long, but she was excited. After graduating at the top of her class from the University of the Philippines, Fe had been offered a full scholarship to study anywhere in the world. She chose Harvard. But in 1936, Harvard didn't accept female students.

Women had been trying to gain admission to Harvard since 1847. The officials who reviewed Fe's application assumed "Fe" was a man. When Fe arrived, the school president realized she was too smart to be sent back home, and Fe del Mundo became the first woman admitted to Harvard Medical School.

Fe was the sixth of eight children; four died when Fe was young. Access to quality health care was limited, and many babies died from treatable illnesses. This inspired Fe to become a doctor. She enrolled in the University of the Philippines at 15 and earned her first medical degree there. Because Fe was tiny (weighing less than 100 pounds), she was advised to pursue pediatrics: the study of children's health. She dreamed of someday building her own children's medical center.

After graduating from Harvard, Fe studied at the University of Chicago, Massachusetts Institute of Technology, and Boston University. But when World War II began, she returned home to help her country. Japan invaded the Philippines and put thousands of people, including children, into internment camps, which were more like prisons. Many children were sick. With the help of the International Red Cross, Fe established a medical center at the University of Santo Tomas called The Children's Home.

Within three weeks Fe and her staff were providing love and comfort to 130 frightened children. Over the next year and a half, Fe cared for 400 children and became known as "the Angel of Santo Tomas."

After the war, Fe opened the first children's hospital in the Philippines, bringing medical care to thousands of rural families. To raise funds to maintain it, she sold her house and belongings and moved into the hospital's second floor. In addition to running the hospital, she published articles and made discoveries that revolutionized pediatric medicine both in the Philippines and around the world.

Dr. del Mundo was still making hospital rounds in her wheelchair at the age of 99; she died a few months before her 100th birthday. She never married or had children; she gave all of her love to her patients. She won many awards, was named the National Scientist of the Philippines, and is recognized as a groundbreaking doctor and humanitarian.

DAME KATERINA TE HEIKŌKŌ MATAIRA

NOVEMBER 13, 1932 – JULY 16, 2011 (TOKOMARU BAY, NEW ZEALAND)

"KO TAKU REO TAKU OHOOHO, KO TAKU REO TAKU MĀPIHI MAURIA."
"MY LANGUAGE IS MY AWAKENING, MY LANGUAGE IS THE WINDOW TO MY SOUL."
—MĀORI PROVERB

It takes only a single generation to lose a language, so if one generation of children grows up without learning and speaking a language, it can be lost forever. Around 6,000 languages are spoken in the world, and linguists (people who study language) believe that within the next century, nearly half will become extinct. When a language disappears, not just words are lost: histories, lullabies, prayers, and jokes vanish too. Thanks to Dame Katerina Te Heikōkō Mataira and her devoted colleagues, we have not said *haere ra* (good-bye) to *te reo Māori:* the Māori language.

The Māori people have lived on the islands of New Zealand in the South Pacific Ocean for hundreds of years. The 19th century brought many new settlers to New Zealand, and by 1840 it was a British colony. One hundred years later, there were a million Pākehā, or non-Māori people, living there. At first, many settlers learned the Māori language so they could trade and negotiate. But eventually, the Pākehā became the dominant population, and English became the primary language. Māori children were discouraged from speaking their own language in school and in public. Speaking English became necessary for survival.

In 1971 a researcher's report confirmed that only 5 percent of the Māori population spoke their mother tongue. The language was dying. Katerina Mataira decided it was time for the Māori people to take matters into their own hands. Katerina was born in Tokomaru Bay as part of the Ngāti Porou tribe. As a teacher and mother she knew education was the key to saving the Māori language and culture. She decided the Māori must set up their own learning institutions, and she dedicated her life to making that happen.

Katerina and her friend Ngoi Pēwhairangi developed a system for teaching *te reo Māori*. They traveled the country recruiting native Māori speakers to become tutors. Soon a network of tutors were teaching the disappearing language to young people and adults. This became a nationwide movement, and Katerina helped found Māori-language immersion schools called Kura Kaupapa Māori. She became known as the mother of the "Kura Kaupapa Movement," and hundreds of these schools are still thriving today. Māori was made an official language of New Zealand in 1987, and a 2013 census reported that 21 percent of native Māori now speak it.

Katerina was also an award-winning children's book writer and the only person to write novels in Māori. In 2011, she received one of New Zealand's highest honors when she was knighted and made a Dame for her service to the Māori language. She died later that year, leaving behind eight children, more than 50 grandchildren and great-grandchildren, a great-great-grandchild, and an enormous legacy.

FAITH BANDLER

SEPTEMBER 23, 1918 (TUMBULGUM, AUSTRALIA) – FEBRUARY 13, 2015 (SYDNEY, AUSTRALIA)

"I WORKED VERY HARD, EVERY DAY OF THE WEEK."

Australia is known for many things: marsupials, the Outback, the Great Barrier Reef. It's not as well known for its civil rights movement, but it should be. Inspired by the activism in America and South Africa, the Australian movement flourished in the 1950s and '60s as Australians fought for the rights of the indigenous Australian people, whose ancestors lived in Australia for thousands of years before Westerners arrived. One of their most beloved leaders was a woman named Faith.

Faith Bandler was born in the small community of Tumbulgum. Her mother was Indian and Scottish, and her father had been born on the tiny island of Vanuatu. When he was 13, he was brought to Australia to work as a slave. Faith and her seven siblings grew up hearing his painful stories, and her parents made sure their children understood the importance of justice.

During World War II Faith worked for the Women's Land Army, picking cherries. Several women she worked with were indigenous Australians, and when Faith learned they were being paid less than her, she was outraged.

That launched Faith's activism: she founded the Aboriginal Australian Fellowship and, together with women like the indigenous activist Pearl Gibbs and feminist activist Jessie Street, built a coalition of students and activists, men and women, both white and indigenous people. Faith knew that unequal pay wasn't the only injustice faced by Australia's indigenous people, who lived in extreme poverty. They had no rights at all: the Australian constitution stated that they shouldn't even be counted in the national census.

In 1957 the Fellowship began a campaign to hold a referendum (or vote) to change the anti-indigenous sections of the constitution. For the next ten years, Faith, who was known for her big smile and convincing speeches, dedicated herself to the cause. Supported by her husband, Hans (a Jewish refugee who had escaped Nazi internment camps), she traveled the country, addressing hundreds of people at churches, trade unions, and schools, speaking passionately about equal rights for all. "I'd get my husband off to work and get my daughter off to school, and I'd attend meetings. I didn't stop," she recalled. She appeared frequently on television and radio, asking her fellow Australians to vote "yes."

The Referendum of 1967 passed with 90 percent of the vote, winning in all six Australian states. The constitution was amended to include the rights of indigenous Australians. And that was only one of Faith's many achievements. In 2000, South African President Nelson Mandela gave her an award "in Honour and Gratitude for a Life of Courageous Advocacy for Justice and for Indigenous People, for Human Rights, for Love and Reconciliation."

LIV ARNESEN AND ANN BANCROFT

LIV: JUNE 1, 1953 (BÆRUM, NORWAY)

ANN: SEPTEMBER 29, 1955 (ST. PAUL, MINNESOTA, U.S.A.)

"WHEN YOU FEEL YOUR HEART BEATING HARD OR YOUR BLOOD RUNNING FAST, YOU HAVE FOUND SOMETHING IMPORTANT. CREATE ROOM FOR IT."

—LIV ARNESEN

The history of Antarctic exploration is filled with stories of brave men who endured harsh elements—never any women. That didn't matter to Liv Arnesen and Ann Bancroft, two little girls who grew up 4,000 miles apart, both dreaming of crossing the icy continent themselves.

When Liv and Ann met in 1998, they were grown-ups who had already set major records in Arctic exploring. Liv skied alone to the South Pole, and Ann was the first woman to cross the ice to the North Pole on foot. But each still yearned to cross Antarctica. Together, they planned the biggest journey of their lives.

Despite all their achievements, they faced criticism. They were told that women don't belong in Antarctica, and one man even felt Ann's bicep to see if she was strong enough (she was)! But Liv and Ann knew they could do it.

They spent two years preparing. "A desire to go to the South Pole is not an impulsive idea," Liv said. "You cannot get the idea in May and set off in October." They would make the trip on skis, with ski sails, each pulling a 250-pound sled containing all their food and gear. To get strong enough to pull the sleds, they tied tractor tires to their waists and practiced pulling them. To get their hands and fingers used to freezing temperatures, they sat inside giant ice-cream freezers and practiced talking on two-way radios!

The trek began in November 2000. Liv and Ann couldn't waste any time. Antarctica's three-and-a-half-month "summer" is the only time it's light and "warm" enough to survive outside. Every day they would wake up, eat, and get onto the ice, snacking hourly to keep up their energy. In the evenings they'd pitch their tents, eat dinner, and read poetry out loud.

The journey was long, painful, and dangerous. On windy days they could cover up to 60 miles, but on calm days they made only six or seven. They had to leap over deep crevasses. Their knees ached, and their toenails fell off. They got sunburns, frostbite, and chapped skin; to warm their fingers they soaked them in oatmeal. They tried to stay positive but sometimes feared they wouldn't make it.

But Liv and Ann knew that their journey was being closely tracked on a website by schoolchildren around the world—three million, to be exact! Thinking of these young people motivated the explorers during their toughest times, and 94 days after they started, Liv and Ann became the first women to cross Antarctica on foot.

Liv and Ann continue to explore the world together, working to educate people about climate change and clean water access. They're committed to showing young people how to make big dreams come true, and they especially want to inspire young girls to explore the world, just like they did.

MIRIAM MAKEBA

MARCH 4, 1932 (JOHANNESBURG, SOUTH AFRICA) – NOVEMBER 9, 2008 (CASTEL VOLTURNO, ITALY)

"I'M GOING TO GO ON SINGING, TELLING THE TRUTH."

Apartheid, a word that means "apart," was a strict form of segregation that kept white and non-white South Africans separate between 1948 and 1994. The world-famous singer Miriam Makeba used her voice to tell the world about it.

When Zenzile Miriam Makeba was just an infant, her mother—a healer and a housecleaner—was caught illegally selling beer, and the two were thrown into prison. Miriam spent the first six months of her life in jail.

Miriam's family was poor, and after her father died she had to work as a domestic servant. But luckily, Miriam had music, which she described as "a type of magic" that helped her through the tough times. Her township was filled with the sounds of African music like *kwela* and *marabi,* and Western styles like big band, gospel, and jazz. At 13 she won a singing contest and began to perform at weddings.

Soon she was touring with several singing groups (always performing separate shows for blacks and whites). In 1959 Miriam got a small part in an anti-apartheid movie. She won an award for her performance and traveled to Venice, Italy, to receive it. This infuriated the South African government. They did not want citizens criticizing their policies. When Miriam tried to return home, she learned that South Africa had canceled her passport. She could not go back. She was in exile.

Miriam was devastated. In London she met the popular singer and activist Harry Belafonte. She traveled to America with him and became an overnight sensation. Before she knew it, she was performing alongside Marilyn Monroe for President John F. Kennedy's birthday in New York City.

A natural performer with amazing vocal range, Miriam drew people in with her emotional delivery. She sang in African languages, and had her own distinct style: she didn't wear makeup, and wore traditional clothes, head wraps, and jewelry. She kept her hair natural, which became known as "the Afro look." In 1967 she became the first black woman to have a Top 10 worldwide hit with "Pata Pata," and she released dozens of albums. In the 1980s her collaboration with musician Paul Simon brought the music and stories of Africa to even more listeners.

Miriam toured all over the world, entertaining and speaking out against injustice. She testified about apartheid in front of the United Nations, and South Africa responded by banning her records and canceling her citizenship. In 1990, activist leader Nelson Mandela was released from prison in time for his 70th birthday. He convinced Miriam to finally return to South Africa, and she did. Her people welcomed her with open arms, calling her "Mama Africa." After she passed away, Mandela told the world, "Miriam's music inspired a powerful sense of hope in all of us."

WANGARI MAATHAI

APRIL 1, 1940 (NYERI, KENYA) – SEPTEMBER 25, 2011 (NAIROBI, KENYA)

"WHEN WE PLANT TREES, WE PLANT THE SEEDS OF PEACE AND HOPE."

Wangari Maathai often told a fable about a hummingbird whose forest was burning. While the other animals watched the fire burn, fearful that they couldn't do anything to stop it, the tiny hummingbird rushed to a stream, sipped a drop of water, and flew to the fire to drop it on the blaze. He did this over and over, and when the other animals told him it was no use, that his tiny droplets would never put out the massive blaze, the hummingbird replied: "I am doing the best that I can." He knew he was tiny, but he believed that doing something to try to solve a problem was better than doing nothing. Wangari encouraged people to "be the hummingbird" and always work to do something.

Wangari and her siblings grew up in a Kenyan village surrounded by lush forests, clear streams, and animals like leopards and elephants living close by. It was a peaceful childhood, and she learned from the land. She valued her classroom education too, and was always at the top of her class.

At the end of high school Wangari was one of 300 Kenyans chosen to receive scholarships to study at American universities. (Another was President Barack Obama's father!) In the United States and Germany she earned degrees in biology, German, and anatomy, becoming the first East African woman to get a PhD. Wangari returned to Kenya, became a professor, raised three children, and was active in international women's rights and environmental organizations. She was also upset by the problems that plagued her country. Kenya of the 1970s was not the Kenya of her childhood: the population had grown, and forests were being cut down to make way for cash crops like coffee and tea. Poverty, unemployment, and malnutrition were on the rise, and Wangari believed the root cause was environmental destruction. As forests were being destroyed for profit, rural communities suffered—and Wangari knew that women suffered the most. They were the primary caretakers, and held great responsibility when it came to tilling the land, planting the food, and feeding the families. Her beautiful country was on the verge of ruin.

So she went to the root of the problem—literally. To empower local women and help restore the environment, she started the Green Belt Movement, which taught rural Kenyan women to nurture and then plant trees to replace the ones being cut down. She showed them how to find seeds for the trees, grow seedlings from them, then plant and care for the trees. Together they created tree nurseries, and the women earned money doing this work, gained job skills, and helped the environment. More trees meant less soil erosion, which meant cleaner water.

CONTINUED

The more Wangari worked, the more she saw the connections between the health of the environment and the health of a country and its people. The Green Belt Movement grew way beyond her expectations. It began with a few women planting trees, and by 2004 more than 30 million trees had been planted by hundreds of women's groups across Kenya. The Green Belt Movement also established a "green network" to share its work with other organizations across Africa.

The Green Belt Movement also encouraged people to register to vote, to speak out for their rights and the environment, and to press for political reform. In 1989, Wangari and her group stood up to the most powerful man in Kenya, President Daniel arap Moi, who wanted to build a 60-floor office building, a parking lot, and a statue of himself in the middle of Uhuru Park, a big, popular park in the capital city of Nairobi. Wangari worked tirelessly to stop the project, writing and speaking about how wrong the plan for the "park monster" was. Her activism angered many who were involved in the project, and the president said she should act like a proper African woman and "respect men and be quiet." Her protests attracted so much media attention that the project was canceled; Wangari had succeeded, but she had also angered many politicians. As is often the case with outspoken, powerful women, Wangari was often dismissed by her critics as "crazy".

During the next decade she continued to expand the Green Belt Movement, and also pressed on as a leading advocate for peace, environmental sustainability, and democracy. She received many international awards from organizations that recognized these efforts, but her own government saw her actions differently; on several occasions she was arrested, beaten, and even put in jail because she was seen as a threat to the men in power.

But Wangari didn't back down: like the hummingbird in her story, she refused to quit. In 2002 she won a seat in Parliament, receiving 98 percent of the vote in her constituency. In 2003 she was appointed Assistant Minister in the Ministry for Environment and Natural Resources.

And in 2004, Wangari Maathai made history when she became the first environmentalist, and the first African woman, to win the Nobel Peace Prize. The Nobel committee praised her "contribution to sustainable development, democracy and peace." This suprised—and upset!—some people who didn't see what her environmental work had to do with "peace." But Wangari's lesson was clear: if we want to care for humans, we must also care for the earth. Though Wangari passed away from cancer in 2011, her legacy lives on. Her family and the Green Belt Movement have set up the Wangari Maathai Foundation to inspire young leaders through the purpose and integrity that marked Wangari's life.

KASHA JACQUELINE NAGABASERA

APRIL 12, 1980 (KAMPALA, UGANDA)

"I'M FULL OF RAGE, BUT I WON'T GET A GUN AND FIGHT. I'LL USE MY WORDS TO BREAK DOWN THE SYSTEM OF OPPRESSION."

It was a teacher who first suggested that Kasha Jacqueline Nagabasera was a lesbian. Young Kasha Jacqueline didn't even know what "gay" or "lesbian" was: she was just being herself. She liked to wear boy's clothes and write love letters to girls.

Wearing "boy's clothes" doesn't make a person gay, but in a culture with strict rules about what boys and girls should and shouldn't wear, it did make Kasha Jacqueline stand out. And because homosexuality is illegal in Uganda, as it is in 38 other countries, this teacher informed the girl and her parents that she had to leave the school.

This discrimination continued for her entire childhood: she was beaten, bullied, and expelled from schools. These experiences made her into the fearless leader she is today. The "Mother of the Gay Rights Movement" in Uganda began speaking out against homophobia in college. At age 23, she founded Freedom and Roam Uganda (FARUG), one of Uganda's main lesbian, gay, bisexual, transgender, and intersex (LGBTI) organizations.

In 2009, the Ugandan government proposed a law making punishments for people suspected of being homosexual much worse; being gay was even punishable by death in some cases. Violent homophobic attacks on LGBTI Ugandans increased, and popular newspapers exposed people who were gay or suspected of being gay. When a paper published pictures of Kasha Jacqueline and her friends, taken without permission, they fought back by suing the newspaper—and won. It was a significant victory, but one of Kasha Jacqueline's close friends, activist David Kato, was killed soon after.

Kasha Jacqueline knew that continuing her fight meant risking her own life, but she had to carry on. She kept working with FARUG, and founded *Bombastic,* an online LGBTI magazine that was downloaded more than two million times in one year. She has testified before the United Nations and appeared on TV and radio, and continues to challenge unjust laws in Ugandan courts. She's been arrested, attacked, and harassed, and moves from house to house, living in secret with friends and supporters.

Kasha Jacqueline is one of the last prominent LGBTI activists living in Uganda; most others have fled the country or been killed. "If we give up now," Kasha Jacqueline asks, "what will happen to the future?"

Kasha Jacqueline has received human rights awards, and in 2015, she was featured on the cover of *Time* magazine's European edition. She traveled to New York City to be the grand marshal of the world's biggest gay pride parade. She loved celebrating there, but she wants the same freedom to love in her own country. And she will not stop fighting for it.

FUNMILAYO RANSOME KUTI

OCTOBER 25, 1900 (ABEOKUTA, NIGERIA) – APRIL 13, 1978 (LAGOS, NIGERIA)

"NO MEMBER OF THE UNION SHOULD THINK HERSELF BETTER THAN THE OTHERS. ALL MUST MOVE FREELY AND HAPPILY TOGETHER."

Francis Abigail Olufunmilayo Thomas was born in the state of Ogun in Nigeria. Her father was a teacher, and education was a top priority in their family; Funmilayo (the name she went by) was the first female student at her elementary school. She then studied in England, and when she returned to Nigeria she became a teacher, too.

The seeds of Funmilayo's activism and leadership were planted in 1932, when she gathered a few young girls and women together to start the Abeokuta Ladies Club (ALC). The ALC was small, and its polite gatherings were focused on learning proper etiquette, drinking tea, and doing crafts.

In 1944, a former student came to see Funmilayo, and introduced her to a market woman who wanted to learn to read. Market women ran the Nigerian markets that were the heart of the region's economy. They traded and sold food, textiles, and other goods and services. Most of the market women were poor and illiterate, and they wondered: could the ALC help them learn to read? Under Funmilayo's direction, the club expanded its membership to include the market women, and began holding literacy classes. But as Funmilayo got to know the new students, she realized illiteracy was not their only obstacle; they also faced daily injustices at the hands of police and government officials.

Nigeria was then a British colony, and the British imposed unfair taxes that were ruining Nigerian businesses. Prior to British rule, the women determined market locations, dates, and prices and decided what goods to trade. Under British policies they were forced to trade goods that no one wanted, and were harassed by officials who seized their products, especially their valuable rice, for no reason. Funmilayo was outraged.

Soon the ladies club that began over tea and sandwiches was an organized political force. In 1945, the members of the ALC held a public press conference to draw attention to the exploitation of women workers. The newspaper ran an article about it, and one week later, the rice seizures stopped. That was just the beginning. The ALC grew to include 20,000 members committed to reforming the country and empowering women. They spoke about education, health care, and the right to vote, and led marches and protests. In 1947, Funmilayo was the only female member of a delegation who went to London to advocate for Nigeria's independence.

The legacy of Funmilayo and the ALC lives on in many ways, including the fact that Funmilayo and her ALC cofounder Eniola Soyinka each raised a remarkable son. Eniola's son, Wole Soyinka, became the first African to win the Nobel Prize for Literature, while Funmilayo's son, Fela Kuti, became a famous musician whose powerful songs told Nigeria's story.

CHIMAMANDA NGOZI ADICHIE

SEPTEMBER 15, 1977 (ENUGU, NIGERIA)

"TO CHOOSE TO WRITE IS TO REJECT SILENCE."

As a child, Chimamanda Adichie loved to read, especially novels by British children's book author Enid Blyton. Young Chimamanda even wrote her own stories based on Blyton's characters—all of whom were white and living happily in the British countryside. Chimamanda, who is Nigerian, had no idea that black Africans "could actually exist" in books. When she grew older, she read books by African writers Chinua Achebe and Camara Laye and realized that girls who looked like her, with dark skin and kinky hair, could be characters in books, too. "As a child, you're not brave enough to change things," she says, "until something makes you realize you can write your own story."

Chimamanda was raised in Nsukka, Nigeria, where the University of Nigeria is located. She and her siblings grew up on the college campus: her father was a professor, and her mother was the first female registrar of the university. Chimamanda was always an outstanding student. She loved science, and her parents encouraged her pursuit of medicine—but she never forgot her love of books and storytelling.

At 19 Chimamanda moved to the United States to continue her education. Her American roommate was excited to meet someone from Africa but had very stereotypical expectations. She couldn't believe Chimamanda could speak English and use a stove, and that she listened to pop music. Chimamanda refers to this as "the danger of a single story"—when we tell only one story about a particular group of people, and expect everyone to be just like that.

While a senior in college, Chimamanda began working on a novel. She was living with her sister and doing childcare and housework in addition to studying. She barely had time to write, so she would wake up at 2 a.m. to work on her book. This hard work paid off: the book, *Purple Hibiscus*, was published when she was only 26, and won many prizes. She has published three more books, including the award-winning novel *Americanah*. Chimamanda's writing refuses to tell a single story: it shows the vast range of what it means to be African, American, black, white, male, and female.

In 2013, Chimamanda was surprised when singer Beyoncé heard a talk she'd given, and asked if she could include a sample on her song "Flawless." In it, Chimamanda offers a definition of something very important to both her and Beyoncé: feminism: "We teach girls to shrink themselves, to make themselves smaller. We say to girls: 'You can have ambition, but not too much. You should aim to be successful, but not too successful. Feminist: a person who believes in the social, political, and economic equality of the sexes." This song became hugely popular, and Chimamanda and Beyoncé are credited with introducing a new generation of young people to the basic ideas of feminism.

HATSHEPSUT

1508 – 1458 BCE (EGYPT)

"NOW MY HEART TURNS THIS WAY AND THAT, AS I THINK WHAT THE PEOPLE WILL SAY. THOSE WHO SEE MY MONUMENTS IN YEARS TO COME, AND WHO SHALL SPEAK OF WHAT I HAVE DONE."

The word *Hatshepsut* means "Foremost of Noble Ladies"—a pretty great name for the first and only female king of ancient Egypt. Hatshepsut was born to King Thutmose I and his queen, Ahmes. When Hatshepsut was young, her father died and she married her half-brother, who had inherited the throne: this made her the most Great Royal Wife, the most powerful queen in Egypt. When her half-brother died, his power was transferred not to Queen Hatshepsut but to her stepson, Tuthmosis III, then just a baby. For the next seven years Hatshepsut ruled on the baby's behalf, along with Tuthmosis. But the determined Hatshepsut had great ambition: she wanted to be king.

Egyptian queens could be very powerful, but it wasn't the same as being the king, who always had the most power. So Hatshepsut declared herself Pharaoh, or king, claiming that her father had wanted her to rule. To help convince the people that she was the rightful king, she ordered carvings to be made on her temple walls that portrayed her as the daughter of not just King Thutmose but also the great god Amun. And she cleverly had herself depicted with the distinct markings of a male king, including a long fake beard and striped headdress. In some depictions she had a woman's body, plus the beard and headdress; in others she had a muscular male body. Everyone knew she was a woman, but the images helped them accept her as king.

Hatshepsut was a successful and peaceful ruler for 22 years. Rather than going to war, she developed positive relationships with neighboring countries. And she was one of the greatest builders in ancient Egypt, commissioning hundreds of construction projects. She restored important monuments and temples, and her huge burial temple is considered one of the greatest works of Egyptian architecture.

Clearly Hatshepsut wanted her legacy to endure and her achievements to be recognized. She had hundreds of statues of herself placed at temples and shrines, and she left detailed accounts of her life in stone carvings. Perhaps she worried that future generations wouldn't believe a woman could rule as she had, or that someone might try to erase her legacy.

After Hatshepsut died, her now-grown stepson became king. And around that time, someone tried to erase all evidence of Hatshepsut's rule. Her name was scratched out of inscriptions on temple walls, her face smashed on many statues. It wasn't until 1903, when an archeologist found her tomb, that her story became known. So the powerful Egyptian women who came after her, like Cleopatra, might not have known about one of Egypt's greatest rulers. Thanks to the efforts of 20th century Egyptologists, Hatsheput's story—and her achievements—have been uncovered.

MADRES DE LA PLAZA DE MAYO

STARTED IN 1977 (BUENOS AIRES, ARGENTINA)

"ONE OF THE THINGS THAT I SIMPLY WILL NOT DO NOW IS SHUT UP."

—MARÍA DEL ROSARIO DE CERRUTI, ONE OF THE MADRES

On April 30, 1977, Azucena Villaflor de Vincento and 13 other women went to the Plaza de Mayo, a public square in the capital of Argentina. They sat on benches clutching their knitting, terrified of being arrested. Gatherings of more than three people were illegal, so when the police told them to move, they began walking around the plaza, two by two. These 14 women were all mothers, and they would continue to meet there every Thursday for the next 38 years, risking their lives and families in pursuit of one goal: to find out what had happened to their missing children.

From 1976 to 1983, Argentina was controlled by a military dictatorship that wanted to eliminate anyone who opposed it. During this time, sometimes known as the "Dirty War," thousands of men and women were taken by the government, disappearing suddenly from homes, offices, classrooms, and streets, never to be seen again. They were called *los desaparecidos* ("the disappeared"): students, artists, professors, activists, social workers, and citizens who had expressed dissatisfaction with the military regime. Even the relatives of those who spoke up were targeted. No one knew whether they were alive or not. The government denied having anything to do with these disappearances, and most citizens were too scared to speak up.

Azucena was a working-class woman; her son, Néstor, and his wife had gone missing. She spent months trying to find them, visiting police stations and government offices. She met other women also searching for their children. Police often laughed at them, saying that their sons and daughters were criminals who had run away. The mothers shared their stories, and, frustrated by the fruitless searches, they decided to act. They selected the Plaza de Mayo, a public square across the street from the presidential palace, for their first demonstration.

The women were taking an enormous risk by appearing publicly, but they found strength in numbers. They marched together, in a large and highly visible group, and each week they were joined by more women. They began wearing white head scarves embroidered with their children's names; the scarves represented the diapers once worn by their children, as well as the white dove of peace. Their chant was simple but powerful: "We want our

CONTINUED

children and we want to be told where they are." Some *madres* brought items belonging to their lost loved ones, and many brought photos or wrote names on large signs.

By the end of the year there were more than 150 *madres* marching each week. They were harassed by the police, but they stuck together. On Mother's Day, they published a letter in a major newspaper. Addressed to the president of the Supreme Court, the military leaders, and the church, it read: "The most cruel torture for a mother is uncertainty about the destiny of her children. We ask for a legal process to determine their innocence or guilt." Then they sent the government a petition with 24,000 signatures and the names of 537 disappeared persons.

The world began to take notice. The United States sent a team to investigate, and when Argentina hosted the 1978 World Cup, journalists reported on the demonstrations. Many professional soccer players joined the *madres* to show solidarity. No one expected a group of grieving mothers to bring international attention to these crimes. The government tried to discredit them, calling them *las locas* (the madwomen), and they also tried to hurt them. The *madres* were beaten and arrested, and three of the founding *madres,* including Azucena, ultimately "disappeared" themselves. But that still didn't stop the women. They opened an office, made their organization official, and traveled around the world, meeting with leaders and human rights groups. "In the plaza we felt strong," they later said. "The plaza made us feel close to our children."

In 1983 Argentina held elections, and the military regime ended. While many of the men responsible for the regime have been imprisoned, the *madres* continue their actions, determined to bring people to justice and to learn what happened to their lost loved ones. Today, anyone who visits the Plaza de Mayo in Buenos Aires will see the ground painted with a great circle of white head scarves, in honor of these courageous women leaders and the strength of their love.

MARTA

FEBRUARY 19, 1986 (DOIS RIACHOS, ALAGOAS, BRAZIL)

"I MIGHT HAVE BEEN SMALL, BUT I WAS A TOUGH LITTLE GIRL."

A dried-up riverbed instead of a grassy field, wadded-up plastic bags instead of a ball, rough boys who didn't want to play with girls. This is how a small yet determined girl named Marta Vieira da Silva learned to play *futebol* ("soccer" in the United States)—and it's how she became Marta, the greatest female soccer player in the world. People in the remote town of Dois Riachos, Brazil, gossiped about Marta, bothered that she wasn't playing with dolls. Her hardworking single mom told her to forget about *futebol,* but she couldn't forget, and she wouldn't stop playing *o jogo bonito* (the beautiful game).

Soccer, the most popular sport in the world, was first introduced to Brazil by the British in the early 1900s. It quickly caught on, and by the 1930s there were many women's teams. Then a new president decided sports were bad for females. In 1941 he issued a decree: "Women will not be allowed to practice sports which are considered incompatible to their feminine nature." This ban remained for almost 40 years, until it was lifted in 1979—just seven years before Marta was born.

At just over five feet tall, Marta always had to play harder, faster, and smarter than the boys who doubted her. She learned how to dribble deceptively, be mentally tough, and go elbow-to-elbow with big defenders. "I remember having to fight just to play," she says. "Some of my teammates thought it was shameful to play with girls." She worked hard, becoming better than the boys, winning tournaments and the attention of coaches and scouts.

At 14, Marta moved to the city of Rio de Janeiro to pursue her *futebol* dreams. She'd had no formal coaching, learning everything on the streets. But she was still one of the best players anyone had ever seen. With supportive coaches she developed even faster and began playing for a women's team.

But women's teams don't make much money, and the leagues often had to shut down. For years Marta bounced around between Brazil, Sweden, and the United States, playing for different teams, scoring goals, and dazzling crowds. She became known as "the female Pelé," after the best player of all time.

Marta caught the world's attention during the 2007 World Cup. In a semifinal game against the United States, the 21-year-old performed a series of moves so dazzling (including scoring a goal) that a video of it went viral and was watched by millions. She was named the FIFA World Player of the Year for five years in a row, more than anyone, male or female. And as a member of the Brazilian national team, she has won two Olympic medals.

QUINTREMAN SISTERS

NICOLASA: DECEMBER 4, 1939 – DECEMBER 24, 2013 (ALTO BIO BIO, CHILE)

BERTA: 1930s (ALTO BIO BIO, CHILE)

"THE LAND IS OUR MOTHER, AND SHE IS ALIVE. WE WILL DEFEND AND FIGHT FOR HER UNTIL THE END."

—NICOLASA QUINTREMAN

Berta and Nicolasa Quintreman belong to the Mapuche people, Chile's largest indigenous group. The Mapuche have lived in the foothills of Chile's Andes Mountains for more than 500 years. The two sisters lived peacefully in their village until the construction of a massive dam threatened their entire existence. Faced with having to leave their sacred land, the elderly sisters resisted. Their quiet fight for dignity launched a new environmental movement.

During the 1980s a big corporation called Endesa wanted to build a 155-foot dam on the Bio Bio, a powerful river that is the ancestral home and economic heart of the Mapuche. Dams are massive structures that block rivers. Not every dam is harmful, but by blocking the flows of rivers, dams can destroy ecosystems. And when large areas of land are intentionally flooded, river-dwelling people are forced to move.

Endesa's dam could be built only if Berta, Nicolasa, and 93 other families in their Mapuche village agreed to leave their land. Endesa promised them new homes, jobs, and money if they did. Some families agreed to the deal, but Nicolasa and Berta refused, even when Endesa offered them over $1 million. The elderly sisters quickly became leaders in the movement and worked to convince other families to stand their ground.

Their resistance was fierce but peaceful. They led marches and testified before congress. Dressed in their traditional colorful Mapuche clothing, Nicolasa and Berta confronted the leaders of Endesa directly. They cited Chilean laws intended to protect the land rights of indigenous people. The demonstrations gained worldwide attention, and the Chilean president and Endesa were embarrassed and angry. No one expected the Mapuche to resist like this—and it went on for over 10 years.

But Endesa continued to pressure them. Police raided the homes of the Quintreman sisters and their neighbors, throwing countless people in jail for defending their land. As the years went by, more families agreed to leave, and the Quintreman sisters felt alone in their struggle. They were growing older, and Nicolasa went blind. In the end, Nicolasa struck a deal with Endesa: she would sell her land in exchange for the release of those being held as political prisoners for their protests.

Although the Quintreman sisters' resistance didn't stop the dam, their efforts had a major impact. Chile's congress strengthened the nation's environmental protections, and the sisters inspired many other indigenous leaders and activists, who have successfully blocked 20 more environmentally damaging energy projects. These two elderly women from an isolated culture leave a legacy of dignity, showing us what it looks like to take a stand for your community and your planet.

POLICARPA "LA POLA" SALAVARRIETA

JANUARY 26, 1795 (GUADAS, COLOMBIA) – NOVEMBER 14, 1817 (BOGOTA, COLOMBIA)

"DO NOT FORGET MY EXAMPLE."

The South American country now known as Colombia was conquered by the Spanish in the 16th century. By the early 19th century, there was tension between those who wanted independence from Spain (the revolutionaries), and those who were loyal to it (the loyalists). In 1817 the Spanish sent troops across the seas, hoping to maintain control of their South American colonies. But a revolution was beginning in Colombia, and it's what Policarpa "La Pola" Salavarrieta lived and died for.

Orphaned as a child, Policarpa lived with her godparents and siblings. They believed in the need for independence and freedom from Spanish rule. As teenagers, she and several of her brothers became active revolutionaries; the boys fought, while she aided the soldiers. She also learned to sew, and found work as a seamstress.

Determined to become more involved in the resistance, Policarpa and one of her brothers sneaked into the capital city of Bogota using forged documents. Thanks to her sewing skills, Policarpa quickly found work in the homes of several loyalists and high-ranking officers. She made dresses and uniforms—and eavesdropped on important military conversations. The seamstress was actually a spy.

Soon Policarpa was a pivotal member of the underground resistance. Nicknamed "La Pola," she collected money, transferred information, and recruited new revolutionaries. This all worked smoothly until she was caught. She was charged with espionage and treason. The Spanish offered her a chance to renounce her activities; she would not, and was sentenced to death.

Her public execution was set for the morning of November 14, 1817. She was brought out with her hands bound, two priests by her side. When offered one last glass of wine, she refused, saying she would take nothing from her enemies. That was just the beginning of her final rebellion: La Pola's tongue was even sharper than her sewing needle.

Instead of repeating the priests' final prayers, she began shouting for all to hear. She cursed the Spanish, predicted their defeat, and declared her love for the revolutionaries. The governor ordered the drummers to player louder to drown out her protests, but she just raised her voice. She insulted the executioners for preparing to shoot a woman, and when ordered to turn her back to the firing squad, she instead turned to face them. "I have more than enough courage to suffer this death and a thousand more," she cried out. "Do not forget my example."

La Pola remains a hero of independence in Colombia. There is a statue of her in Bogota, and her face is on currency and stamps. November 14, the day of her death, is known as "The Day of Colombian Women."

BASTARDILLA

(COLOMBIA)

"EVEN WHEN I'M NOT PAINTING, I'M THINKING OF THE THINGS I'M GOING TO MAKE."

The streets of Bogota, Colombia, have long been notorious for violence, gangs, and drugs. But thanks to the work of people like Bastardilla, they're now known for something else: art. As one of the best-known female street artists in Bogota—and the world!—Bastardilla creates big, beautiful public paintings that brighten the landscape, and send powerful messages.

Bastardilla translates to "italics": it's a pseudonym, or fake name, which is common in the street-art world. Even as a small child, Bastardilla knew she wanted to become a painter. But for many years she would throw out her artwork after creating it. She wanted to share it with others but didn't know how. Then she realized the answer was all around her: in the streets of Bogota, where anyone could experience the power of art for free. Using cheap tools and paint, she began painting on any outdoor surface she could find. To reach the tops of high walls, she attached paintbrushes to long poles, dipping them carefully in buckets of paint. Bastardilla's signature style includes thick wavy lines, and she often throws glitter onto the wet paint so her pieces sparkle at night!

Bastardilla prefers to remain anonymous because she wants the focus to be on her artwork, not her image. She bases her work on what she sees: as a Colombian woman, she has witnessed violence and poverty, but also strength, beauty, and the power of nature. Almost all of her work depicts women: women crying, working, lying down, even breaking a rifle in half. Her paintings also capture the effects of the violence that has long plagued her country. "I like being able to see and work with those subjects which aren't often seen," she explains. "The resilience of women, the way their stories of strength can be found on any given corner." The street-art scene is very male-dominated, but women like Bastardilla are changing that. Other female street artists in Bogota include Remedios, Zas, Zurik, LeDania, and Perversa.

One of Bastardilla's most powerful pieces is on the side of a house in an impoverished neighborhood. It depicts a native Colombian woman holding up the roof. She carries small children strapped to her body. The word "Minga!" is written next to her, referring to a group of indigenous Colombians who lead peaceful protests to bring attention to environmental issues. The house that the woman holds up can be seen to represent the earth, and Bastardilla reminds viewers that women carry the weight of the world, as well as the promise of the future.

Bastardilla has created murals in Berlin, London, New York, and Mexico. She doesn't accept money for her work, and her pieces always carry strong messages, like her tribute to Rosa Parks in London, and her painting in Mexico that honors students who've been the victims of gang violence.

NANNY OF THE MAROONS

APPROXIMATELY 1685 (GHANA) – APPROXIMATELY 1755 (JAMAICA)

"NANNY AND THE PEOPLE NOW RESIDING WITH HER AND THEIR HEIRS ARE GRANTED . . . A CERTAIN PARCEL OF LAND."

(FROM A 1739 TREATY)

The island of Jamaica has seven national heroes. The lone woman among them is Nanny of the Maroons, though most Jamaicans refer to her simply as "Nanny." A remarkably skilled fighter, leader, and healer, Nanny became a powerful symbol of Jamaica's resistance against slavery and colonialism.

Jamaica was colonized by the Spanish in the 15th century, and the Spaniards brought many slaves from West Africa. In 1655, the British came and successfully fought the Spanish for control of the small island. Many of the enslaved Africans took advantage of the chaos and fled high up into the jungle-filled mountains. They were known as "Maroons," and they built rebel villages there. The newly free Maroons were able to return to many of the cultural and spiritual practices of their home countries, growing crops, hunting animals, and trading. They also developed their own militias in order to fight off the British, who wanted to recapture the Maroons and continue their slave-dependent economy.

Of the many Maroon leaders, Nanny is one of the most remarkable. It is generally believed that Nanny was born in Ghana, in western Africa, as one of the Ashanti people. She was then taken (along with her four brothers) from her village and brought to Jamaica to work on sugar plantations. As young slaves in Jamaica, Nanny and her brothers were inspired by the Maroons, and when they finally escaped, they headed up into the mountains to join them. Nanny and her brother Quao founded a village in the Blue Mountains, on the eastern (or windward) side of Jamaica. Nanny quickly emerged as the leader, and eventually the village became known as Nanny Town.

Nanny was an excellent strategist who knew how to outsmart the British troops. She taught her people how to camouflage themselves with sticks, leaves, and mud, and how to set decoys in the jungles. She was a practitioner of Obeah (a kind of folk magic and religion), and she created an image of herself as a mystical woman with magical powers. This intimidated the British, who heard rumors that she could stop bullets with her bare hands!

Under her leadership, the people of Nanny Town farmed and traded peacefully with neighboring Maroon villages, and helped almost 1,000 slaves escape to freedom. Nanny Town and the Windward Maroons thrived and grew to the point that the government officially awarded Nanny the land. It is not known how or when Nanny died; some say she was killed by a British captain, but other legends claim she died of old age.

Nanny remains an important figure in Jamaica. In 1976 the government declared her a National Heroine, and Jamaicans are reminded of her on a regular basis: her portrait is on the Jamaican $500 bill (about $5 US), which people often call a "Nanny."

SOR JUANA INÉS DE LA CRUZ

NOVEMBER 12, 1651 (TEPETLIXPA, MEXICO) – APRIL 17, 1695 (MEXICO CITY, MEXICO)

"WHAT THEN IS THE EVIL IN MY BEING A WOMAN?"

Most people, even those we consider geniuses, are educated in school. They learn from teachers, in classrooms and study halls. But one of Mexico's most brilliant minds was quite different: Sor Juana Inés de la Cruz was totally self-taught. For a young girl growing up with a single mother in 17th-century Mexico, that's a pretty remarkable feat.

Sor Juana was born Juana Ramirez during the time of Spanish colonial rule. As a very young girl she sneaked books from her grandfather's library and taught herself to read and write. By age three she could read and write in Latin; by five, she knew complex math; by eight, she was writing poetry. By the time she was a teenager she knew Greek logic and had learned to write in Nahuatl, an Aztec language. Desperate for more education, she begged to be allowed to disguise herself as a boy so she could attend college.

Soon Sor Juana caught the attention of regional leaders, who couldn't believe the stories they heard about this gifted girl. The viceroy (a leader who represents the king) assembled a group of leading scholars to test her intelligence. At 17, Sor Juana appeared before these esteemed men. They quizzed her on literature, science, mathematics, and philosophy, and she answered every question correctly.

Amazed, the viceroy offered to support Sor Juana financially so she could continue to study and learn. She entered a convent and became a nun because she longed "to have no fixed occupation which might curtail my freedom to study." In the peace of the convent, Sor Juana pursued her true passions: reading, writing, and studying.

Sor Juana wrote plays, poems, and stories, which the viceroy had published in Spain. She wrote everything from romance to comedy to religious texts, and collected a library said to have been the largest in the New World. One of Sor Juana's key themes was knowledge, and how important it was for women to have access to it.

But her supporters wanted Sor Juana to focus only on religious writing and to leave the philosophical and political ideas alone. In response, she wrote what is considered her most famous text: *Respuesta a Sor Filotea,* or "Answer to Sister Filotea." In this letter Sor Juana passionately defends the right of all women to learn and study. She notes famous educated women from history, and echoes the words of St. Teresa of Avila with the comment: "One can perfectly well philosophize while cooking supper." This letter is considered the first feminist text of the New World.

Sor Juana's former convent is now a university that bears her name, and her face appears on Mexican coins and paper currency.

FRIDA KAHLO

JULY 6, 1907 – JULY 13, 1954 (COYOACÁN, MEXICO)

"I AM HAPPY TO BE ALIVE AS LONG AS I CAN PAINT."

It seems like everyone today knows who Frida Kahlo is, but that wasn't always the case. Like so many women artists throughout history, Frida didn't gain the recognition she deserved until many years after her death. When she died in 1954, the *New York Times* obituary headline read "Frida Kahlo, Artist, Diego Rivera's Wife." This was how she was known for a long time: as the strange wife of famous muralist Diego Rivera. She's now considered one of the greatest artists of the 20th century.

Magdalena Carmen Frieda Kahlo y Calderón was born just before the outbreak of the Mexican Revolution. She lived in La Casa Azul, a small house that her father painted blue. When she was six she came down with polio, which left her right leg permanently disfigured. To help it heal, her father encouraged her to exercise and play sports, but she always had a prominent limp.

Frida didn't plan to be an artist—she wanted to be a doctor, and she studied medicine at one of Mexico's finest schools. Everything changed when she was in a bus accident at age 18. She was severely injured and spent months in a full-body cast. Isolated and in pain, she began to paint. Her mother made her an easel she could use while lying down, and her father shared his oil paints. She experimented with bright colors that reminded her of traditional Mexican folk art. The small self-portraits that she created helped her process her traumatic accident.

Frida eventually showed four of her pieces to the artist Diego Rivera, whom she adored. "You've got talent," he told her, and it was true. Her paintings were deeply personal, yet they combined elements of Mexican art, classical European painting, and newer Surrealist works. She and Diego eventually married and became part of a thriving Mexican art scene. It was a male-dominated scene but Frida also encountered women like singer Chavela Vargas, muralist Fanny Rabel, and photographer Lola Alvarez Bravo (the first and only person to exhibit Frida's paintings in Mexico during her lifetime).

Frida remained relatively obscure until the 1980s, when a biography about her got people's attention. Feminist and Latina artists began to celebrate her work, and she became a cultural icon, now more well-known than Diego. Frida's life was painful, and she created over 140 paintings that reflected it. Unlike many other artists at the time, Frida didn't paint landscapes or abstract shapes: she painted her real, pained self. She celebrated her flaws, her fears, her country, and her desires and she did it beautifully.

QUEEN LILI'UOKALANI

SEPTEMBER 2, 1838 – NOVEMBER 11, 1917 (HONOLULU, HAWAII)

"YOU MUST REMEMBER NEVER TO CEASE TO ACT BECAUSE YOU FEAR YOU MAY FAIL."

Until the 19th century, the Hawaiian Islands were ruled by powerful chiefdoms (called *ali'i*), and the Hawaiian people had their own religion, economy, and language. There was no such thing as private property; the land was a living relative, the place where ancestors dwelled. Hawaii is also where Lydia Lili'u Loloku Walania Wewehi Kamaka'eha, also known as Queen Lili'uokalani, was born and raised. The first and only queen of the Kingdom of Hawaii, Lili'uokalani fought hard to save her kingdom and her culture.

In 1778, British sea captain James Cook arrived in Hawaii. Soon more British came, and then Americans, eager to make money by growing crops like sugar. Before Captain Cook there were one million native Hawaiians; by the 1840s, fewer than 100,000 had survived the diseases the nonnatives had brought. And as the (predominantly white) businessmen gained more economic power, they wanted political power, too.

Lydia was born in Honolulu and adopted into a high-ranking royal family. She was a well-educated and gifted poet and musician who studied European and American music, as well as traditional Hawaiian songs. She wrote songs and poems, and loved to sing. At age 39, she was named crown princess of the Kingdom of Hawaii and began to go by her royal name of Lili'uokalani.

The American businessmen were becoming more aggressive in their desire to control Hawaii. In 1887 they forced King Kalākaua to sign a new constitution that stripped the Hawaiian people of their sovereignty, or power. Lili'uokalani was furious. When the king died, she became the first woman ever to rule Hawaii.

Queen Lili'uokalani's first act as queen was to rewrite the constitution. Threatened by her bold moves, the businessmen decided to overthrow her. Backed by the U.S. Navy, they forced Lili'uokalani to surrender the Hawaiian Kingdom to the United States. She was arrested and imprisoned in 'Iolani Palace, her own home. She wasn't allowed to read, but she did have paper and pencil. Her story was eventually published as *Hawaii's Story by Hawaii's Queen,* making her the first published Hawaiian woman. While imprisoned, she composed some of her greatest songs, including the famous love song "Aloha 'Oe."

Lili'uokalani was no longer queen, but she had won the hearts of the native Hawaiians. She never gave up the fight for sovereignty. When she died, Hawaii mourned; she left all of her money to Hawaiian orphans and destitute children. In 1959 the United States did ultimately make Hawaii a state. And in 1993, 76 years after Lili'uokalani's death, the U.S. government finally apologized for the unlawful overthrow of the Hawaiian Kingdom.

VENUS AND SERENA WILLIAMS

VENUS: JULY 17, 1980 (SAGINAW, MICHIGAN, U.S.A.)

SERENA: SEPTEMBER 26, 1981 (SAGINAW, MICHIGAN, U.S.A.)

"MY MOM RAISED US TO BE STRONG WOMEN."
—VENUS WILLIAMS

The Southern California sun beat down on a concrete tennis court, where an African-American man raised a racquet, then swooped it down fast. He repeated the motion until the two young sisters watching from the bench yelled, "I got it, Daddy! I can do that!" The sisters were Venus and Serena Williams, and they were in Compton, a crime-ridden city not far from Hollywood. Sometimes gunshots rang out in the distance; the girls knew how to drop to the ground to avoid stray bullets.

Taught by their father, Richard, who learned how to play tennis by studying instructional videos, and their mother, Oracene, who homeschooled them, Venus and Serena played and worked hard. Their parents saw their circumstances as an advantage. Growing up in a place like Compton, they said, there's only one place you can go: up. The world-champion sisters have redefined the game of tennis with their talent, bravery, and refusal to apologize for who they are, where they come from, and where they want to go.

The girls started playing at age four. Venus (big sister by 14 months) and Serena were both naturals, with athletic bodies and amazing instincts. By age 10, Venus was the top young player in Southern California. Word spread about the tennis prodigies from the streets of Compton, and in 1991 the Williams sisters were featured in *Sports Illustrated*. They each turned pro at age 14.

As African-American females in a historically white and European-dominated sport, Venus and Serena got attention—but not all of it was positive. They didn't fit the traditional tennis mold. They were muscular and aggressive, and they used unique footwork and techniques. They wore bright outfits and beads in their hair. Inspired by African-American tennis trailblazers like Althea Gibb and Arthur Ashe, Venus and Serena held their heads high and focused on being the best players in the world. "When anyone is critical of what I do, I'm just motivated by it," explains Venus.

They rose through the ranks, winning game after game. They've both been ranked #1 in the world, and each has won four Olympic gold medals. As two of the world's top players, they've ended up playing *against* each other in many key tournaments. This hasn't been easy for the sisters, who are close. It's no wonder they've won 13 Grand Slam titles playing doubles!

Venus and Serena are more than tennis players; they're fashion designers, actors, entrepreneurs, and activists. For years the French Open and Wimbledon—two of the world's biggest tennis tournaments—paid female winners less prize money than male winners. Venus led a campaign to change that, and in 2007 both tournaments gave in. And the first woman to win that equal Wimbledon prize money? Venus, of course, who won the trophy and was paid the same amount as tennis champ Roger Federer.

BIRUTĖ MARY GALDIKAS

MAY 10, 1946 (WIESBADEN, GERMANY)

"ALMOST EVERY DAY, ORANGUTANS TEACH ME SOMETHING NEW."

It began with *Curious George*. The woman who has devoted her life to the study of orangutans was once a young girl in Toronto, Canada, and the classic book about the little monkey was the first book she checked out of the library. Birutė Galdikas was fascinated by George and his companion, the Man with the Yellow Hat. She wanted to spend time with primates, just like him! She checked out more books about primates. The humanlike eyes of an orangutan caught her attention, and she knew she was born to work with these mysterious animals.

Birutė went on to study zoology and psychology, attending graduate school at UCLA, in California. In 1969, at 23, she learned that Dr. Louis Leakey, a famous anthropologist, was coming to speak at her school. Leakey had chosen two young female scientists to go into the wild to study primates, the closest living relatives of humans: Dian Fossey worked with gorillas, and Jane Goodall studied chimpanzees. Birutė wanted to be the third primate researcher. After his lecture, she boldly approached Dr. Leakey; he agreed to interview her and immediately saw her deep commitment. He needed someone to study orangutans, because scientists knew almost nothing about them. So Birutė and her husband headed off for one of the world's most remote places.

Orangutans live only on the Southeast Asian islands of Borneo and Sumatra. When Birutė arrived, these areas were very wild and sparsely populated. Many people doubted that Birutė would even be able to *see* an orangutan, because they're such solitary creatures. She set up Camp Leakey, a tiny outpost in a remote rain forest. There were no phones, roads, or mail, but there *was* plenty of danger, including leeches, poisonous insects, and poachers.

The orangutans did appear. Birutė embarked on a long process of slowly gaining their trust. She recorded every single movement and sound the orangutans made, and four years after her arrival she published a cover article in *National Geographic*, revealing her groundbreaking research. Camp Leakey is now the top orangutan research and rehabilitation center in the world, and Birutė has worked there for 44 years.

The three women that Dr. Leakey selected became known as "The Trimates," and are now considered the founding mothers of primatology. Birutė is also an international environmental activist, working to raise awareness about the endangered orangutans. The forests of Borneo and Sumatra are being burned to make way for palm tree plantations for palm oil, and the orangutans are highly threatened. In 1986 Birutė established the Orangutan Foundation International. She is committed to saving these animals from extinction, stating, "I rack my brains every single day for how to help them more."

BUFFY SAINTE-MARIE

FEBRUARY 20, 1941 (PIAPOT PLAINS CREE FIRST NATION RESERVE, SASKATCHEWAN, CANADA)

"I WAS A JOURNALIST WITH A GUITAR."

Buffy Sainte-Marie was born on the Piapot Reserve in Canada. Her birth parents were Cree, the largest of the First Nations tribes ("First Nations" is the term used to refer to Canada's indigenous people), but Buffy was adopted by American parents and raised in Massachusetts.

She always had a gift for music. At four she taught herself to play piano, and she was always making up songs. When she got a guitar for her 16th birthday, she didn't know how to tune it, so she twisted the knobs until it sounded like the music in her head. And then those songs came pouring out. (Her unique tuning style later inspired her friend, folksinger Joni Mitchell.)

After she graduated from college in the 1960s, she returned to the reservation where she was born to reconnect with her Cree heritage and family. She performed her songs in coffeehouses in Toronto and New York, alongside singers like Bob Dylan and Leonard Cohen. Her voice had a distinctive warbly vibrato, and her lyrics were political. Her song "Universal Soldier" became an instant anthem of the anti–Vietnam War movement. Buffy was the first Native performer many people had ever seen or heard, and she made a point to educate them about the lives and suffering of Native people.

In 1964 Buffy's career took off, and she was named "Best New Artist" by *Billboard Magazine*. Many of her songs became hits for other singers, including Elvis Presley and Janis Joplin. Some of her songs spoke out against war; others decried government theft of Native lands. Buffy didn't know it at the time, but President Lyndon B. Johnson, and later President Nixon, put her on a secret list of artists "to be suppressed." The list was given to radio stations, who decided not to play her songs. For years her music was played on radio stations in countries all over the world but not in the United States.

In 1975, Buffy got a phone call from the producers of *Sesame Street,* the most popular children's television show in the world. They wanted her to recite the alphabet like most celebrity guests, but Buffy wanted to do more. "Have you done any Native American shows?" she asked the producers. Buffy saw an exciting educational opportunity: to show children that Native people still exist. Buffy joined the show's diverse cast for five seasons, traveling to Native American reservations, singing songs about diversity, and even breastfeeding her baby while Big Bird looked on.

Buffy continues to work for native visibility and rights, environmental justice, and peace. She's performed in many countries, won numerous awards, and started several nonprofit organizations dedicated to educating and empowering Native and other children. In 2015, at age 74, she released her 20th album to great acclaim.

ENIAC PROGRAMMERS

HIRED IN 1945 (U.S.A.)

"I BELIEVED I COULD LEARN AND DO ANYTHING AS WELL AS ANYONE ELSE."

—JEAN JENNINGS BARTIK, ENIAC PROGRAMMER

On February 15, 1946, the U.S. Army unveiled a massive machine to the public. It was 80 feet long and 8 feet tall, and was covered in more than 3,000 switches, wires, and cables. It was the ENIAC (Electronic Numerical Integrator and Computer): the first all-electronic programmable computer. The audience watched in awe as the machine performed a set of math calculations that would have taken humans weeks to do. The *New York Times* ran the headline "Electronic Computer Flashes Answers, May Speed Engineering." The ENIAC and its inventors became famous. But there was something missing from all the articles about it: the names and faces of the six young women who programmed the entire machine.

Jean Jennings Bartik, Marlyn Wescoff Meltzer, Ruth Lichterman Teitelbaum, Betty Snyder Holberton, Frances Bilas Spence, and Kay Mauchly Antonelli came from different cities and backgrounds, but they had a few things in common: they were young American women who had gone to college, who loved math, and who were eager for adventure and opportunity.

In 1945 they each saw advertisements like this one: "Wanted: Women With Degrees in Mathematic . . . Women are being offered scientific and engineering jobs where formerly men were preferred. Now is the time to consider your job in science and engineering." These ads were made by the U.S. Army, and were placed in newspapers and math journals all over the country. Jean, Marlyn, Ruth, Betty, Frances, and Kay all jumped at the chance to get a job like this, and were among the 100 women hired by the army to work at the University of Pennsylvania as "human computers."

World War II was raging, and the army needed these "computers" to do repetitive math equations to calculate how far missiles would go, and where they would land. These calculations were done by hand, and could take weeks to solve—the women spent their days scribbling numbers

CONTINUED

on huge sheets of paper. The army wanted the calculations to happen faster, so they started a top-secret project called ENIAC.

Once the machine had been built, the engineers needed people to program it. The engineers thought it would be an easy job, so they decided to recruit women to do it: Betty, Jean, Marlyn, Ruth, Frances, and Kay were selected. They were referred to as "the ENIAC girls" and their task was initially described as "setting up" the ENIAC. But what they did was far more important than merely setting something up—what they did revolutionized computer programming.

The "girls" were given very little information about what the machine was and what it would be used for. They weren't even allowed to see it, because it was so classified. As Kay Mauchly Antonelli explained: "Somebody gave us a whole stack of blueprints . . . and they said, 'Here, figure out how the machine works and then figure out how to program it.'" There was no operating manual or existing programming language, yet the women programmed the entire machine. They studied the blueprints and diagrams, breaking big problems into small steps. They also figured out how to troubleshoot it, including devising a system to pinpoint which of the 18,000 vacuum tubes was burned out. They worked together on the project for months, and when it was time for the public demonstration, they were finally allowed to actually see and touch the machine. For two weeks straight they worked harder than ever to program it to perfection, often staying at work until midnight to solve last-minute glitches. It's because of their hard work that the February 1946 audience got to see that amazing, successful display.

All of the ENIAC programmers remained in the field of computer science for the next several decades, working as early programmers and software designers. This was remarkable because many American women who worked during WWII left the workforce once the war was over. Betty Snyder Holberton—who was once told by a math professor that she'd be better off staying home to raise children—went on to help design the software of the first commercial computers, alongside Jean Jennings Bartik.

Despite all their accomplishments, the six women went completely unacknowledged until 1997 when Betty, Jean, Marlyn, Ruth, Frances, and Kay were inducted into the Women in Technology International Hall of Fame, and were finally honored as some of the world's first digital programmers.

GUERRILLA GIRLS

FORMED IN 1985 (U.S.A.)

"IT'S LIKE HAVING A SUPERPOWER."

In 1984, the Museum of Modern Art in New York City announced a new show featuring the most important art in the world. Out of 169 artists exhibited, only 13 were female. Seventeen countries were represented, but almost all the artists were white. A group of female artists noticed this but they weren't surprised, as that's how it was at *every* major museum. They formed a protest outside the museum, but were largely ignored.

So the women got creative. They started making bold, eye-catching posters, fliers, and stickers that called out and exposed discrimination in the art world. They assumed the names of dead women artists (like Käthe Kollwitz, Zubeida Agha, and Alice Neel) and began wearing gorilla masks when they appeared in public. That's right—gorilla masks!

Guerrilla is a Spanish word that describes a kind of freedom fighter. After someone confused the spelling of *guerrilla* and *gorilla,* it was suggested the women dress like giant apes. They bought hairy black masks, and realized how effective a silly disguise could be. Soon *everyone* was talking about the Guerrilla Girls and their powerful messages. They were the feminist superheroes of the art world!

The Guerrilla Girls sneak around at night, pasting their black-and-white posters all over the walls of cities. They appear in front of museums, wearing their masks and talking to people about equal representation. They even make huge billboards. The Guerrilla Girls like to use humor in their images, but they also include facts to support their arguments. In the Metropolitan Museum of Art they found that 5 percent of the artists were women, but 85 percent of the nude paintings and statues were of females. That led to their most famous billboard: a classic female nude with a gorilla mask on her head, and the slogan "Do women have to be naked to get into the Met Museum?"

When they first started out, some people dismissed the Guerrilla Girls as jealous wannabe artists. But the vast majority appreciated their bold actions. Soon major artists and the media were celebrating them, and museums and galleries began realizing the importance of showing a diverse range of artists. When asked why gender and racial equality in art matters, a Guerrilla Girl known as "Frida Kahlo" replied, "How can you really tell the story of a culture when you don't include all the voices within the culture? Otherwise it's just the story and history of power."

There have been about 60 members of the Guerrilla Girls over the years. They've created 90 posters, actions, billboards, postcards, and books that call out gender and racial bias in art, film, politics, and pop culture. Much has changed since the Guerrilla Girls started their work, but there is a lot more to be done—that's why they're still going strong today!

GRACE "GRANUAILE" O'MALLEY

1530 (CONNAUGHT, IRELAND) – 1603 (ROCKFLEET CASTLE, CLARE ISLAND, IRELAND)

"THERE CAME TO ME A MOST FAMOUS FEMININE SEA CAPTAIN CALLED GRACE O'MALLEY . . . WITH THREE GALLEYS AND 200 FIGHTING MEN."

—FROM A LETTER WRITTEN BY LORD DEPUTY SIR HENRY SIDNEY, 1577

Little Grace O'Malley (also known as Gráinne or Granuaile) wanted nothing more than to sail with her father, an Irish sea captain, and his fleet of ships. The O'Malleys were a powerful seafaring family on Ireland's west coast. Two of their castles, Clare Island and Kildawnet, on Achill Island still remain today. Grace begged her parents to let her go to sea, but her mother insisted it was no place for a girl. So, according to legend, Grace cut off her long red hair and dressed in boys' clothes. In the 1530s, that wasn't exactly a normal way for a girl to behave. But that was how Grace O'Malley, who would soon become Ireland's most notorious pirate, operated!

At age 16, Grace married an Irish chieftain and they had three children. But Grace wasn't the type to stay at home. After her father's death she took command of his fleet and when her husband died, many of his clansmen joined her. Trading as far away as Spain and Portugal, with some piracy and plundering on the side, Grace gained a reputation as a daring sea captain.

The seas were filled with traders and pirates, and the land was ruled by chieftains fighting to protect their clans from the neighboring English, who were slowly but steadily taking over Ireland. One by one the chieftains surrendered, but Grace held out, determined to remain free and to protect her family and followers. The English were not amused; they sent an army to capture her, but she escaped and led her people in rebellion against the English. This was around 1588, when she was almost 60 years old!

The English kidnapped her youngest son and falsely accused him of treason, a crime punishable by death. To save her son, Grace put her own life at risk and went right to the most powerful person in England: Queen Elizabeth I. Elizabeth's subjects were shocked when the queen agreed to meet with the pirate! They spoke in Latin, their only language in common. Grace told the queen of her family's suffering at the hands of the queen's generals in Ireland and asked her to spare her son. The queen ordered his release from prison and gave Grace her personal permission to continue to sail the seas.

Grace lived into her 70s, a remarkable age for a woman in the 16th century. She made such an impact that countless legends survive: how she fought off an attack by Turkish pirates the day after giving birth, how she proposed marriage to her second husband because she wanted his castle, and how a year later she divorced that husband by saying, "I dismiss you."

Whether or not these tales are true, historical records show that Grace O'Malley was a brave sea captain, pirate, political strategist, chieftain, mother, wife, and daughter who defied gender expectations as well as the might of England.

PRINCESS SOPHIA DULEEP SINGH

AUGUST 8, 1876 (ELVEDEN, SUFFOLK, ENGLAND) – AUGUST 22, 1948 (BUCKINGHAMSHIRE, ENGLAND)

"IF I AM NOT A FIT PERSON FOR THE PURPOSES OF REPRESENTATION, WHY SHOULD I BE A FIT PERSON FOR TAXATION?"

The early life of Sophia Duleep Singh was typical for a 19th-century princess in Britain. She sipped tea with her godmother, Queen Victoria; bred champion dogs; and was photographed wearing fancy clothes from Paris. However, she and her family were in Britain only because her father, Maharajah Duleep Singh, heir to the Sikh kingdom, had been overthrown by the British and exiled to England. Sophia was content in her comfortable life—until she and her sister took a secret trip back to India, where she saw, for the first time, life beyond the palace grounds.

In India, Sophia witnessed inequality. She met struggling families, impoverished children, and people fighting for India's independence. Newly aware of these negative effects of British colonial rule, Princess Sophia returned to England transformed. She left her socialite life behind and used her wealth and popularity to make a difference. She established homes for lascars (poor Indian sailors who were treated like slaves) and sent aid to the Indian freedom fighters.

Then she met Christabel and Emmeline Pankhurst, the mother and daughter leading the suffrage movement (the fight for women's right to vote). Sophia joined the fight and started selling copies of *The Suffragette* newspaper—right outside the British royal palace! She publicly refused to pay her taxes until she could vote, and became the biggest single donor to the Women's Social and Political Union (WSPU), the leading militant group campaigning for women's suffrage, led by Christabel and Emmeline. The WSPU used aggressive tactics to get their message across: they broke windows, held hunger strikes, even set buildings on fire. On November 18, 1910, Sophia and Emmeline led a march that became known as "Black Friday" after the hundreds of participants were beaten by police. When Sophia saw a woman being attacked, she stepped right between her and the violent officer. He recognized the royal princess and ran away.

The outbreak of World War I put a hold on the British suffrage movement. Sophia continued her activism, tending to wounded Indian soldiers and collecting money for them. To the soldiers she treated, Princess Sophia was a hero, but to the British royalty, she remained a disgrace. How could a princess dress in common clothes, sell newspapers on the sidewalks, and march through the streets? Why was she interacting with Indian soldiers? Sophia knew the answer: she was fighting for equality.

Women got the right to vote in Britain in 1928, and Sophia's travels to India helped fuel the suffrage movement there (it took until 1950 for all Indian women to be able to vote). Princess Sophia Singh defied what a princess *should* be, and showed Britain and India—and the world—what a princess *could* be.

POLY STYRENE

JULY 3, 1957 (BROMLEY, ENGLAND) – APRIL 25, 2011 (SUSSEX, ENGLAND)

"I STARTED WITH NOTHING BUT A FEW MELODIC LYRICS AND A LOT OF DETERMINATION."

In 1976, a British band called The Sex Pistols performed the first ever punk rock concert. This legendary show was loud and sweaty, and in the crowd was a young woman celebrating her 19th birthday. Her name was Marianne Elliot-Said, and she wanted to be a singer. She'd been writing song lyrics since she was 12. As she watched the man onstage sing wildly, she thought: *I can do this too!*

She placed an ad in a British music magazine, headed "YOUNG PUNX WHO WANT TO STICK IT TOGETHER!" Several musicians responded, and soon they'd started a punk band: X-Ray Spex. She chose the stage name "Poly Styrene" because it was "plastic and synthetic." After just six rehearsals they played their first gig at the Roxy, a famous punk club in London. They were a hit. Overnight Marianne became Poly, and X-Ray Spex became a game-changing punk band.

Poly's mom was Scottish-English, and her father had come to England from the African country of Somalia, speaking little English. When Poly was a child her mother moved them from the mostly white suburb of Bromley to the more racially diverse town of Brixton; she felt it would be a less judgmental place for Poly to grow up.

Poly was a creative, adventurous kid who loved to play dress-up. She traveled around England by herself at age 15, and on returning, opened a small clothing shop where she sold funky clothes and developed her distinctive fashion sense. She wore military hats, mismatched jewelry, and the brightest colors she could find. She chose baggy clothes because she didn't want people to focus on her body shape.

The British punk scene was often angry and dreary—and dominated by white men. Poly was radically different: a mixed-race teenage girl with a huge smile that showed off her silver braces. She sneered the opening lines of her first hit song ("Some people say little girls should be seen and not heard!") and went on to prove that idea very wrong. She sang about consumerism, sexism, and unfair beauty standards, and she used humor and sarcasm to get her point across. For Poly, punk rock was about "young people getting up and doing something, creating something." It was a way for her to express her emotions and ideas.

X-Ray Spex became very popular, very fast. But the fame was overwhelming, and after a few years Poly grew tired of it all. She left the band, had a daughter, and focused on her spiritual practice. She kept making music throughout her life; her final album was released the day after she passed away from breast cancer at age 53. In the brief life of X-Ray Spex, they became one of the most popular punk bands ever. Poly has been an inspiration to singers like Kim Gordon, Kathleen Hanna, Beth Ditto, and many more.

SOPHIE SCHOLL

MAY 9, 1921 (FORCHTENBERG, GERMANY) – FEBRUARY 22, 1943 (MUNICH, GERMANY)

"WHAT WE DID WILL CAUSE WAVES."

Sophia Magdalena Scholl was like lots of other German girls her age: she was proud of her country, and in 1933, at twelve years old, Sophie joined the League of German Girls—the girls' wing of the Nazi Party. The Nazis were in control of Germany; led by Adolf Hitler, they had formed a racist and deadly government. They hated Jewish people, gay people, black people, Communists, and many others. Those who didn't agree with them were criticized and excluded—or even killed.

But like many Germans, especially the young people, Sophie didn't yet know about the cruel things her government was doing. She was just excited to be part of the group that all her friends and siblings were in. As she and her brother Hans grew older, though, the power of the Nazis, and the horror of their acts, became apparent. The parents of Sophie and Hans had raised them to be independent, curious thinkers, and they both began to question the truth about their government.

Hans went to the University of Munich, and Sophie soon followed, planning to study biology and philosophy. She and Hans and their friends began to learn more about what the Nazis were actually doing. They read reports of the mass killings of Jewish people, and atrocities committed in other countries. They also read philosophers who wrote about civil disobedience and the importance of following your conscience. All their lives these young people had been taught that their government was the greatest, but now they were learning that they had been fooled. They loved Germany, and they came to hate the Nazis.

Sophie, Hans, and their friends had to be very secretive about their conversations. The Nazi secret police, the SS, spied on everyone, and even saying something like "I don't like Hitler" could get you arrested (that actually happened to Sophie and Hans's father). But the more they talked and read, the more they learned—and they knew they had to act. At first Hans and his friends wanted to keep Sophie out of their plan, but they realized how smart and committed she was. They also knew that, as a girl, she was less likely to be stopped by the SS, who could search people at any time.

The group called themselves "the White Rose," and in 1942 they wrote an anonymous one-page essay criticizing the Nazis. They made hundreds of copies, and Sophie bravely scattered the leaflets all over the university campus, leaving them outside of classrooms for students and teachers to find. This was one of the first times that anyone in Germany had dared to print negative statements about the Nazis. Some students turned in the leaflets to the SS, but many kept them and made more copies. Using a hand-operated copier, Sophie and the White Rose made five more leaflets—more than 9,000 copies in all—

CONTINUED

getting bolder with each one. The second leaflet began: "Why do the German people behave so apathetically in the face of all these abominable crimes?"

They quoted the Bible, as well as famous philosophers like Aristotle and Goethe, and at the bottom of each flier they printed: "Please make as many copies of this leaflet as you can and distribute them." They mailed them to cities all over Germany, and called for the German people to resist their own government, and to reject Hitler. The fourth leaflet ended with the words "We will not be silent. We are your bad conscience. The White Rose will not leave you in peace!" The phrase "We will not be silent" became their unofficial motto. They didn't limit themselves to the leaflets alone: they also made stencils that said "DOWN WITH HITLER" and "FREEDOM!" and they snuck out at night to graffiti these words all over the walls of Munich. The leaflets and graffiti quickly caused a sensation: the SS were furious, and they began a desperate hunt for the perpetrators.

On February 18, 1943, Sophie and Hans were distributing their sixth leaflet. They still had fliers left when the bell was about to ring, and Sophie didn't want to waste any. She ran to the top of a stairwell, and threw an armful of papers into the air. As they floated down to the students below, a custodian spotted Sophie and Hans—and turned them in. They were arrested and interrogated. They confessed and took full responsibility, refusing to name any other White Rose members. Despite that, several more members were arrested. They were all charged with treason, and sentenced to death. Sophie was 21 years old.

Sophie was calm throughout her entire trial. "Somebody, after all, had to make a start," she declared to the Nazi judge. "What we wrote and said is also believed by many others. They just don't dare to express themselves as we did." In the middle of the trial, Sophie and Hans's father tried to enter the courtroom. The guards forced him outside, but everyone heard him shout: "One day there will be another kind of justice! One day they will go down in history!" Sophie held her head high and defended her peaceful actions, proclaiming "I did the best that I could do for my nation. I therefore do not regret my conduct and will bear the consequences." Hans's last words were "Long live freedom!" Sophie's were "The sun still shines."

Several months after their execution, a copy of the final leaflet was smuggled out of Germany and given to the Allies, who air-dropped millions of copies over Germany. It was titled "Manifesto of the Students of Munich." Sophie and the White Rose became famous for their immense courage and commitment to peaceful resistance in the face of tyranny.

MARIE CURIE AND IRÈNE JOLIOT-CURIE

MARIE: NOVEMBER 7, 1867 (WARSAW, POLAND) – JULY 4, 1934 (HAUTE-SAVOIE, FRANCE)

IRÈNE: SEPTEMBER 12, 1897 – MARCH 17, 1956 (PARIS, FRANCE)

"I SPENT MY BIRTHDAY ADMIRABLY. I MADE AN X-RAY OF A HAND LOADED WITH FOUR RATHER LARGE SHELL FRAGMENTS."

—LETTER FROM IRÈNE CURIE TO MARIE CURIE, 1916

Irène Joliot-Curie didn't spend her 18th birthday opening gifts or dancing with friends. She spent it on a World War I battlefield, training doctors in a Belgian field hospital to use the new X-ray machines to help save soldiers' lives. The portable machines were called *petites Curies* after their inventor: Irène's mother, the world-famous scientist and first woman ever to win a Nobel Prize, Marie Curie.

Irène and her mother had always been close. When Marie was busy traveling or working in the lab she mailed math problems home to Irène, who tried hard to impress her mom by solving the challenging equations. When at home, Marie tutored Irène and her sister, Ève, and she started a rotating home school called the Cooperative with several of her colleagues (some of France's most famous thinkers and scientists).

When World War I began in 1914, Irène was headed to college, and Marie—already famed as a scientist—was opening her own research institute in Paris. Both had to put their plans on hold. Marie sent the girls to the seaside to be safe with family and devoted herself to inventing mobile X-ray units that could save lives. Before X-rays, doctors had to use their hands, eyes, and best guesses to locate bullets and shrapnel in wounded soldiers' bodies. X-rays allowed for successful surgeries and less infection. The problem was how to get these machines onto the battlefield. Marie located a car, scavenged 500 pounds of equipment to build the first mobile unit, and assembled teams of volunteers to train doctors.

Irène wanted desperately to join her mother. On August 1, 1914, the day French troops mobilized, Marie wrote to Irène: "You and I, Irène, we will try to make ourselves useful." Irène came to Paris, enrolled in nursing classes, and joined her mother in a brave adventure. Field hospitals were set up all over France and Belgium, and Marie and Irène traveled to them with the *petites Curies*. Irène, just a teenager, often went alone. The doctors weren't always excited to see a teenage girl arrive at their hospitals. But once they realized what she could do, they listened. And learned. Irène later said, "My mother had no more doubts about me than she had about herself."

After the war, both continued their research and studies. During the war years, Irène had also attended university classes and between 1915 and 1917 she received degrees from the Sorbonne in math, physics, and chemistry. Irène met and married another scientist, Frédéric Joliot, and in 1935 they won the Nobel Prize in Chemistry, making Irène and Marie the only mother-daughter duo to both win the award. Continuing the family tradition, Irène and Frédéric's two children, Hélène and Pierre, both became famous scientists, too.

JOSEPHINE BAKER

JUNE 3, 1906 (ST. LOUIS, MISSOURI, U.S.A.) – APRIL 12, 1975 (PARIS, FRANCE)

"NOT EVERYBODY HAS THE SAME COLOR, THE SAME LANGUAGE, OR THE SAME CUSTOMS, BUT THEY HAVE THE SAME HEART, THE SAME BLOOD, AND THE SAME NEED FOR LOVE."

The first time Josephine Baker danced in public she was on a street in St. Louis, Missouri. It was 1919, and she was a 13-year-old black girl who'd dropped out of school and left the one-room shack she shared with her mom. Josephine had been working as a servant since she was eight, so she was used to hustling for money. Dancing was more fun, though, and she was good at it. By age 15, she was performing on the vaudeville circuit, and then in New York City. She was energetic and funny and knew how to charm and entertain an audience. By 19 she'd caught the eye of a talent scout, who offered her the opportunity to dance in Paris, France, as part of an all-black dance troupe. Eager for something new, Josephine said yes.

On October 2, 1925, she took to the stage in Paris, and was an instant hit. She wore skimpy outfits and danced with wild abandon. Jazz was brand-new to Paris, and Josephine did popular dances like the Charleston. Her most famous dance was done wearing a skirt made out of bananas. She was beautiful but also silly, often crossing her eyes and making goofy faces while she danced. Josephine quickly became the most famous performer in Europe, and huge crowds came to see her wherever she performed, thrilled by everything from her dance moves to her iconic hairstyle. In 1934, she became the first black woman to star in a major motion picture, *Zouzou*.

Josephine became rich and famous. The once-homeless girl could now afford to buy designer clothes and even a pet cheetah named Chiquita (who wore a diamond collar). But she didn't use her money and fame just to buy fancy things: for her entire life, she used her celebrity to make a difference. She loved her new country of France and became a citizen. When World War II broke out, she volunteered for the Red Cross. And then she became a spy for the French Resistance.

As a popular entertainer, Josephine was able to move freely around Europe despite the war, performing at clubs, fancy parties, and embassies. She charmed high-ranking Japanese, Italian, and Nazi officials who never suspected she might be acting as an informant. She eavesdropped on their conversations and passed the information on to French and British intelligence. As she traveled around to Spain, Portugal, North Africa, and England, she smuggled strategic information about Nazi troop locations and airfields by writing in invisible ink on her sheet music, and pinning secret notes to her underwear! After the war, France awarded her a medal for her bravery.

But Josephine wasn't done: her next battle was racism. She was shocked that she could travel freely around Europe and the rest of the world, being treated as an equal human being, but be refused service

CONTINUED

at restaurants back in America and called terrible names. In the 1950s, she did a U.S. tour, and her contract said she would not perform in segregated venues. This led to public battles and the desegregation of clubs in cities like Miami and the notoriously racist Las Vegas (where even stars like Nat King Cole and Ella Fitzgerald were barred from renting nice hotel rooms). When a Vegas club refused to let black ticket-holders in, Josephine declared, "I'm not going to entertain," and she sat down on the stage until the owners gave in. In 1963, she was the only woman to speak alongside Dr. Martin Luther King Jr. at the famous March on Washington. She wore her French military uniform and her medal of honor, and spoke to the massive crowd about her own struggle for justice.

Josephine's commitment to racial equality was so deep that she adopted 12 children from different parts of the world, including Korea, Israel, Morocco, Finland, Colombia, and Algeria. She wanted to show that "children of different ethnicities and religions could still be brothers." Josephine, who spoke four languages, called her family "the Rainbow Tribe," and allowed visitors to tour their home (a 15th-century French castle!) to observe how happy the big multiracial family was.

Josephine Baker was the first black woman to be an international celebrity—but she was much more than that. She was a soldier, a spy, a writer, an activist, a mother, and a passionate advocate for equality, love, and peace. She was also a fashion icon, a trailblazer, and an inspiration for generations of performers, from Shirley Bassey and Diana Ross to Tina Turner and Beyoncé.

MARIA MONTESSORI

AUGUST 31, 1870 (CHIARAVALLE, MARCHE, ITALY) – MAY 6, 1952 (NOORDWIJK, NETHERLANDS)

"CHILDREN ARE HUMAN BEINGS TO WHOM RESPECT IS DUE."

In 1907, in a poor neighborhood outside of Rome, Italy, a young woman opened a preschool. Of the 50 students, some were shy, some were wild, and none had ever known anything like Casa dei Bambini, the first school started by Maria Montessori. Their teacher observed them carefully. She knew that the students were in fact teaching her.

As a child, Maria loved school and received high marks in her classes. She especially loved the sciences, and at age 13, she entered an all-boys technical school to study engineering (she also studied botany, math, drawing, chemistry, physics, literature, zoology, and several foreign languages).

A career in engineering was unusual enough for a woman, but after graduation she shocked everyone, especially her father, when she announced that she wanted to go to medical school. This was considered impossible, and she was rejected from several schools. Eventually the University of Rome accepted her. She was harassed by male classmates and not allowed to participate in dissections with them; she had to stay after hours and do the work alone. Despite that, she won academic prizes and graduated as the first female doctor in Italy.

One of Maria's roles as a doctor was to visit asylums for children with mental illnesses, who were considered "insane" or "feeble-minded." Maria was horrified by the treatment of these children, who received no stimulation or love. What did these children need? How could they learn? To find out, she began doing research. Soon she was creating her own system of education for all children, not just ones with learning challenges. She called it the Montessori Method.

Maria believed that every child has the ability and desire to learn, and that this spirit should be encouraged. She also believed that children can teach themselves, and in order to do that they must have freedom to explore. Maria thought that playtime *was* learning time. She developed specific activities, objects, and toys that would stimulate learning. She also introduced radical new ideas about the role of teachers, who, she said, were there to guide and learn from children—not just tell them what to do.

It wasn't long before her ideas caught on. In 1913, she traveled to America, where prominent people like Alexander Graham Bell, Helen Keller, and Thomas Edison all praised her work. She traveled the world to train teachers in person, and she helped start thousands of Montessori schools. She was nominated three times for the Nobel Peace Prize, and was the first and only woman to appear on Italian money. She wrote numerous books and gave countless lectures, and her methods are used today in more than 22,000 Montessori schools in 110 countries.

HYPATIA

BETWEEN 350 AND 370 – MARCH 8, 415 (EGYPT)

"RESERVE YOUR RIGHT TO THINK, FOR EVEN TO THINK WRONGLY IS BETTER THAN NOT TO THINK AT ALL."

The brilliant teacher stood in the center of the city dressed in a traditional cloak, speaking with authority about the ideas of philosophers like Plato and Aristotle. The students crowded around, eager to absorb the knowledge of this illustrious speaker. Her name was Hypatia, and she was one of the greatest mathematicians, astronomers, and philosophers of her era. At a time when women were mostly confined to their homes and considered property, Hypatia's life was extraordinary.

She was born in the city of Alexandria, Egypt, which was then ruled by the Greeks. It was a vibrant city of culture and learning, and one of its most important institutions was the Museum, a kind of university whose library held more than a half-million scrolls. Many great thinkers taught at the Museum and were developing new ideas about medicine, physics, biology, astronomy, and geography.

One of them was Hypatia's father, Theon of Alexandria. When Hypatia was born, he devoted himself to teaching her all he knew. They developed a strong bond, working together to study and write "commentaries" about classic texts. Writing a commentary meant that you read the works of someone else and wrote your own thoughts and ideas about it. Theon saw how brilliant his young daughter was, and soon her knowledge had surpassed his.

She began writing her own commentaries and giving lessons to students in her home, which became a gathering place for her devoted followers. She wrote texts about algebra and geometry, expanding on existing theories and coming up with new ones. She was also an inventor: she came up with designs for a number of scientific instruments.

When Hypatia started giving public lectures about philosophy, word spread about this remarkable woman. She went out in public, wearing scholars' robes instead of traditional women's clothes; she even drove her own chariot. Soon the city officials were consulting with her on important city business. Many men wanted to marry Hypatia, but she refused, preferring to focus on her work.

Her lessons and talks were incredibly popular—but not with everyone. Tension was building in the region, as different groups fought for power. Some of the powerful people began to dislike mathematicians. They said they were tricksters, or even witches. The Museum and its library were eventually destroyed, and in 415 CE, the brilliant Hypatia, the first known female mathematician and scientist, was killed by an angry mob who felt threatened by her advanced scientific ideas. Though her life was cut short, her ideas and inventions lived on for centuries, influencing great thinkers like Sir Isaac Newton and René Descartes.

EMMA GOLDMAN

JUNE 27, 1869 (KOVNO, RUSSIA) – MAY 14, 1940 (TORONTO, CANADA)

"I WANT FREEDOM, THE RIGHT TO SELF-EXPRESSION, EVERYBODY'S RIGHT TO BEAUTIFUL, RADIANT THINGS."

At 5:30 a.m. on a freezing December day in 1919, a barge left Ellis Island in New York City, headed for Europe. The 249 people on board were being deported because of their political beliefs. As the barge sailed past the Statue of Liberty, a woman peered out of a porthole. She had come there 34 years prior, seeking freedom and liberty. And now, because of her commitment to these very ideals, she was being sent away. Her name was Emma Goldman.

Emma was born in the Russian Empire, in the small city of Kovno (now Kaunas, Lithuania). Her Orthodox Jewish family faced anti-Semitism. Her father could be abusive, and when he lost his job, Emma and her sisters had to work in factories to make ends meet. Young Emma was headstrong: she didn't like following rules, and got in trouble at school for speaking her mind. She dreamed of a better life, inspired by the strong women she read about, from the biblical figure Judith, who took revenge on her enemies, to Vera Pavlona, a fictional heroine of Russian literature who was a free-thinking independent woman. At 15, Emma's father arranged a marriage for her. When she begged to return to school instead, he threw her books into the fire and declared that "girls do not have to learn much!" That was it. In 1885, 16-year-old Emma and her big sister, Helena, escaped the violent poverty and growing anti-Semitism and fled to America.

Emma soon joined thousands of other immigrants who'd traveled to New York City, living in crowded slums and working in factories. She worked 11 hours a day and made $2.50 a week; it was more "American nightmare" than "American dream." The factory conditions were terrible, and Emma felt the workers were being exploited. She had always held strong opinions, but her political awakening came when she learned about the Haymarket Affair: a group of activists were falsely accused of a bombing in Chicago, and then hanged. The news of this injustice changed Emma's life: "I had a distinct sensation that something new and wonderful had been born in my soul," she wrote. "A great ideal, a burning faith, a determination." The energetic Emma was ready.

In New York she met like-minded activists, and began to publish her writing and give lectures. She believed in anarchy, or the abolition of government, capitalism, and private property, and thought that people—especially women—should be able to love who they want, have children when they want, and move through the world freely.

In the 1890s Emma worked as a nurse and midwife in the tenement slums of New York's Lower East Side, tending to poor immigrant women. The conditions were cramped and unsanitary, and some women did not survive childbirth. Many

CONTINUED

of the women begged Emma to help them get birth control, which was hard to find, especially for poor women. Emma saw that women needed access to birth control to be truly free. Her lectures on this topic were well-attended, and soon she was smuggling contraceptives into the United States when she returned from abroad. This violated the 1873 Comstock laws, which made writing or publicly speaking about birth control illegal, and Emma was arrested at least twice. She recruited others to help her, including a young nurse named Margaret Sanger. Emma became Margaret's mentor and supporter: Margaret wrote articles for Emma's magazine *Mother Earth*, and Emma wrote for and sold copies of Margaret's paper *The Woman Rebel*. Margaret went on to lead the fight for reproductive rights and founded the organization that would eventually become Planned Parenthood.

While Emma was serious about her causes, she was also a free-spirited, fun-loving woman. Once she was at a party with other prominent activists, and a young man scolded her for dancing. As the leader of the anarchist movement, he said, she shouldn't be having fun in public, as her "undignified behavior" might hurt their cause. A furious Emma told him to mind his own business, and defended her right to live with joy. She believed that "the way one lived one's life every day was the most powerful political statement," and Emma was committed to living with passion as well as purpose.

In 1919 Emma spoke out against the military draft for World War I. For this, she was stripped of her citizenship, and forced to return to Russia, along with hundreds of others. After leaving the Soviet Union she moved to Sweden, then Germany. She traveled the world speaking, writing, and spreading her radical ideas of social change and equality. A prolific writer, she penned numerous articles, essays, and pamphlets, as well as thousands of personal letters. Her five books include *Living My Life*, her two-volume, 1,000-page autobiography. Emma was never one to stand idly by while injustice occurred. She joined the fight wherever she went, and was a true radical woman.

THE STATELESS

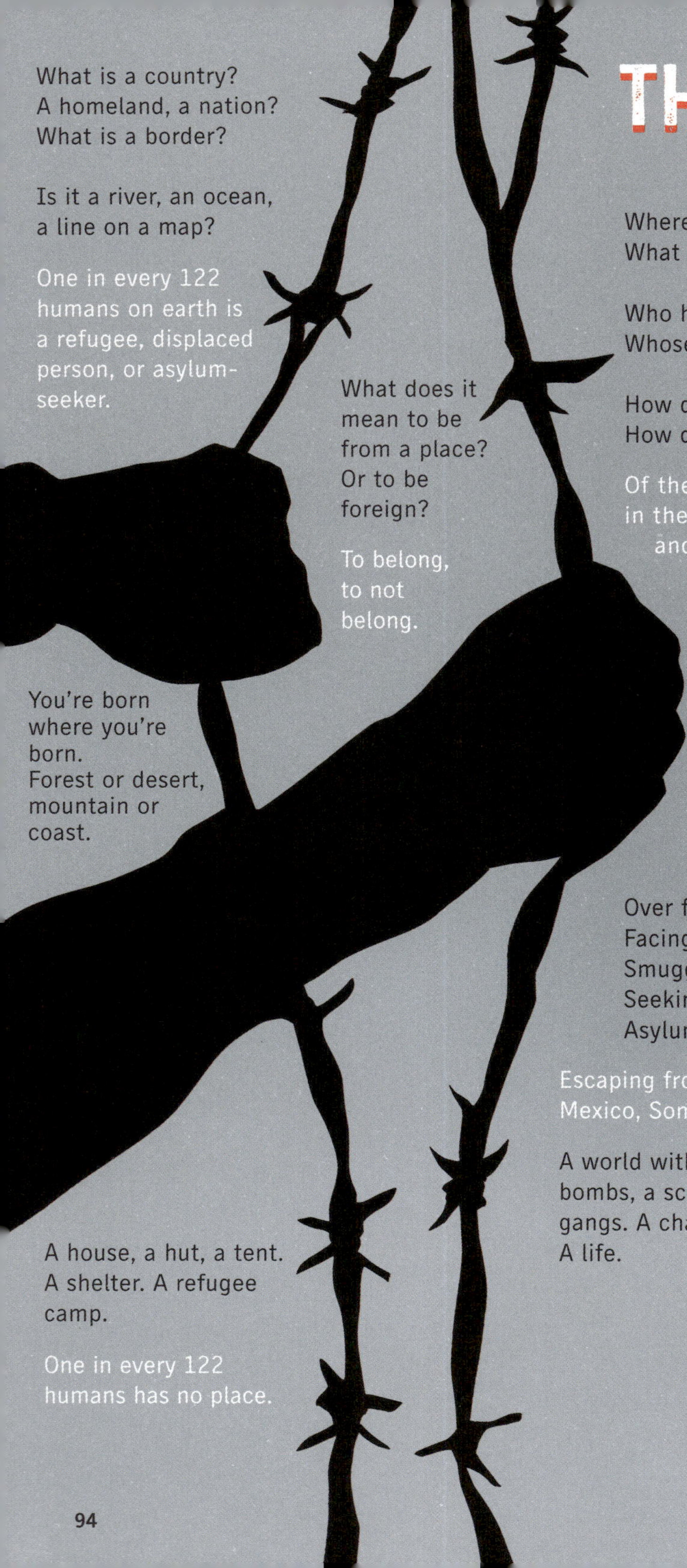

What is a country?
A homeland, a nation?
What is a border?

Is it a river, an ocean,
a line on a map?

One in every 122
humans on earth is
a refugee, displaced
person, or asylum-
seeker.

You're born
where you're
born.
Forest or desert,
mountain or
coast.

A house, a hut, a tent.
A shelter. A refugee
camp.

One in every 122
humans has no place.

What does it
mean to be
from a place?
Or to be
foreign?

To belong,
to not
belong.

Where did you come from?
What body, what people?

Who holds you there?
Whose mouth speaks your language?

How did I get here?
How did *you* get there?

Of the 60 million forcibly displaced people
in the world, almost 80 percent are women
and children. They leave their homes,
cities, and countries due to war,
violence, discrimination, hunger,
environmental catastrophe.

Immigrant. Refugee.
Migrant. Homeless.
Placeless. Stateless. Human.

They've fled Eastern Europe,
Northern Africa, the Middle East,
South Sudan, Central America.

Over fences, underground.
Facing soldiers, police, militias.
Smugglers, traffickers, border patrol.
Seeking safety, food, education.
Asylum, acceptance, citizenship.

Escaping from Burma, Syria, Afghanistan, Eritrea.
Mexico, Somalia, Turkey, Ukraine. Guatemala, Iraq.

A world without war, a night without
bombs, a school without guns, a day without
gangs. A chance. A home.
A life.

They say good-bye to friends, families, schools, and jobs, and set out in the hope that somewhere, somehow, they will find a new place. Sometimes they leave with their entire families; sometimes husbands and fathers have been lost to war, to fighting.

Millions of mothers walk in the cold dark, babies on backs and children in arms.

They soothe them in boats as they cross black seas, sing lullabies in tents in dangerous camps.

They flee while pregnant, give birth on roads, cradle new hope. They keep going.

Will they turn her away?
Is there room on the land?
In our hearts?

Forced out of Ireland, Congo, Germany, Cuba. Have to leave Palestine, Serbia, Vietnam, Cambodia.

They pass babies over fences, into someone else's hands.

Send daughters across deserts, away from the wars they're born into.

Cross deserts and oceans to new lands.

And sometimes, they arrive at train stations and airports to eager crowds with shoes and coats.

Meals and toys, diapers and books, signs that say *Welcome* in unfamiliar languages.

Classrooms and books, the chance to dream, to have a future.

What does it mean to help, to accept?

To be a friend, a neighbor, a sister?

No human being is illegal.

Who belongs? Who helps? We do.

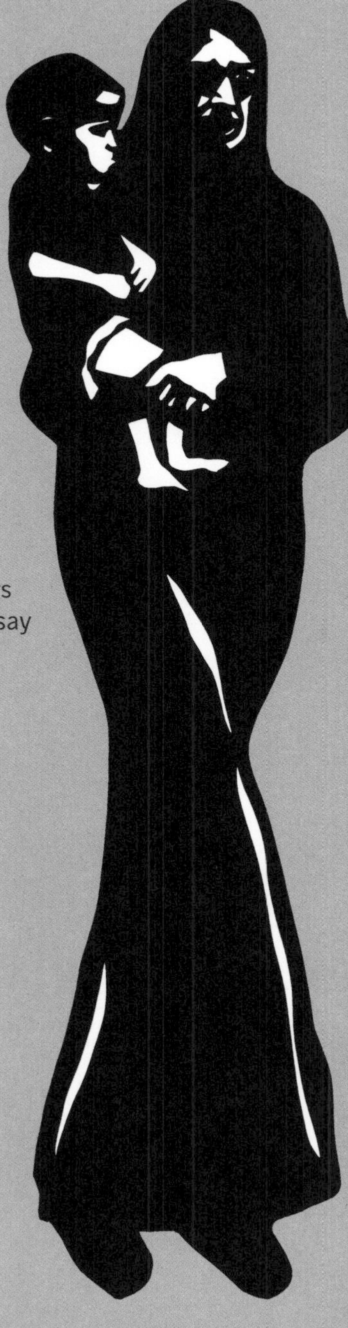

MORE RAD WOMEN WORLDWIDE

This book tells 40 stories from 30 countries. There are almost 200 countries in the world—it could easily be 40,000 stories! Here are 250 *more* rad women from all over the world for you to check out:

AFGHANISTAN

Tahmina Kohistani
Olympic Athlete

Malalai Joya
Writer and Activist

ALBANIA

Urani Rumbo
Teacher and Playwright

ALGERIA

Dahia al-Kahina
Resistance Leader

Assia Djebar
Filmmaker

ANGOLA

Nzingha
Queen

ANTIGUA

Jamaica Kincaid
Writer

ARGENTINA

Eva Perón
Politician

Maria Lugones
Philosopher

ARMENIA

Hayganush Mark
Poet and Author

Zabel Yesayan
Novelist

AUSTRALIA

Layne Beachley
Surfer

Oodgeroo Noonuccal
Poet

Doris Pilkington Garimara
Author

AUSTRIA

Hedy Lamarr
Actor and Inventor

Anna Freud
Psychiatrist

Rosa Welt-Straus
Women's Rights Activist

BAHRAIN

Ruqaya Al-Ghasra
Olympic Athlete

BANGLADESH

Begum Rokeya
Feminist Social Worker

Pritilata Waddedar
Revolutionary

BELARUS

Svetlána Alexiévich
Investigative Journalist

BELGIUM

Alexandra David-Néel
Spiritualist and Adventurer

Diane von Fürstenberg
Fashion Designer

Luce Irigaray
Philosopher

BERMUDA

Dame Lois Browne-Evans
Lawyer and Politician

BOLIVIA

Silvia Lazarte
Indigenous Leader

Bartolina Sisa
Resistance Fighter

Julieta Paredes
Activist and Organizer

BOSNIA

Jasmila Žbanić
Filmmaker

BOTSWANA

Unity Dow
Judge and Human Rights Activist

BRAZIL

Bertha Lutz
Zoologist, Feminist, and Politician

Ana Néri
Nurse

Isabel
Princess

Leticia Bufini
Skateboarder

BULGARIA

Dimitrana Ivanova
Women's Rights Activist

BURMA

Wai Wai Nu Rohingya
Activist and Political Prisoner

BURUNDI

Ketty Nivyabandi
Poet and Activist

CAMBODIA

Ros Sereysothea
Singer

Indradevi
Queen

CANADA

Kenojuak Ashevak
Artist

Anna Mae Aquash
Activist

Roberta Bondar
Astronaut

Manon Rhéaume
Hockey Player

CAPE VERDE

Cesária Évora
Singer

CHILE

Gabriela Mistral
Poet

Isabel Allende
Author

Ana Tijoux
Rapper

María Teresa Ruiz
Astronomer

CHINA

Zheng Shih
Pirate

Dowager Cixi
Empress

Jin Xing
Dancer

Dr. Flossie Wong-Staal
Molecular Biologist

COLOMBIA

Gaitana
Rebellion Leader

COSTA RICA

Emma Gamboa
Educator

Pancha Carrasco
Soldier

CUBA

Alicia Alonso
Ballerina

Ana Mendieta
Artist

Ana Betancourt
Activist

Lydia Cabrera
Anthropologist

CZECH REPUBLIC

Božena Némcová
Writer

Martina Navratilova
Tennis Player

Bertha von Suttner
Nobel Peace Prize Winner

DEMOCRATIC REPUBLIC OF THE CONGO

Neema Namadamu
Disability and Women's Rights Activist

DENMARK

Lili Elbe
Transgender Artist

DOMINICAN REPUBLIC

The Mirabal Sisters
Political Activists

ECUADOR

Matilde Hidalgo
Activist and Politician

EGYPT

Neithhotep
First Queen

Nawal El Saadawi
Writer

Doria Shafik
Feminist Leader

Umm Kulthum
Singer

ENGLAND

Boudica
Queen

Aphra Behn
Playwright

Cecilia Payne
Astronomer

Jane Marcet
Chemist

ETHIOPIA

Taytu Betul
Queen

FIJI

Virisila Buadromo
Activist and Leader

FINLAND

Tove Jansson
Artist and Writer

Rosina Heikel
Gynecologist and Midwife

FRANCE

Christine de Pizan
Medieval Author

Olympe de Gouges
Feminist Author

Agnès Varga
Filmmaker

Claude Cahun
Artist

THE GAMBIA

Fatou Bensouda
Lawyer

GERMANY
Emmy Noether
Mathematician

Dr. Ruth Pfau
Nun and Leprosy Doctor

Fanny Mendelssohn
Composer

Hannah Arendt
Philosopher

GHANA
Yaa Asantewaa
Warrior Queen

GREECE
Aspasia
Writer and Teacher

Cynisca
First Olympic Athlete

Sappho
Poet

Kallirhoe Parren
Women's Rights Activist

GUAM
Cecilia Cruz Bamba
Senator and Organizer

Clotilde "Ding" Castro Gould
Storyteller

GUATEMALA
Rigoberta Menchū
Indigenous Activist

María Josefa García Granados
Journalist

HAITI
Edwidge Danticat
Writer

Anacaona
Chief

Yvonne Sylvain
Doctor

HONDURAS
Elvia Alvarado
Human Rights Activist

HUNGARY
Margit Slachta
Social Activist

Ilona Zrínyi
Freedom Fighter and Countess

ICELAND
Björk Guðmundsdóttir
Musician

Bríet Bjarnhéðinsdóttir
Women's Rights Activist

Jóhanna Sigurðardóttir
Former Prime Minister

INDIA
Arundhati Roy
Author

Vandana Shiva
Environmentalist

Sampat Pal Devi
Women's Rights Advocate

Mary Kom
Boxer

INDONESIA
Cut Nyak Dhien
Guerrilla Leader

Kartini
Educator and Feminist

Megawati Sukarnoputri
Politician

Ayu Utami
Writer

IRAN
Táhirih
Poet and Mystic

Shirin Ebadi
Lawyer and Activist

Shirin Neshat
Filmmaker

Maryam Mirzakhani
Mathematician

IRAQ
Nazik Al-Malaika
Poet

Zaha Hadid
Architect

IRELAND
Bernadette Devlin
Politician

Mairead Maguire
Peace Activist

Anna Haslam
Suffragist

ISRAEL
Amal Elsana Alh'jooj
Bedouin Activist

Ada Yonath
Chemist

ITALY
Catherine of Siena
Saint and Scholar

Sofonisba Anguissola
Painter

Francesca Caccini
Composer

Rita Levi-Montalcini
Neurologist

JAMAICA
Stafanie Taylor
Cricket Player

Mary Seacole
Nurse

Grace Jones
Singer

JAPAN

Yayoi Kusama
Artist

Tazuko Sakane
Filmmaker

Murasaki Shikibu
First Novelist

Tomoe Gozen
Samurai

JORDAN

Fadia Faqir
Novelist

KENYA

Tegla Loroupe
Olympic runner
and Humanitarian

KIRIBATI

Teresia Teaiwa
Poet and Scholar

KOREA

Seondeok
Queen

Yoo Kwan-soon
Independence Leader

Na Hye-sok
Feminist Poet and Artist

KUWAIT

Fatima Al Qadiri
Musician

LEBANON

Nazira Zain al-Din
Feminist Writer

Fairouz
Musician

LIBERIA

Angie Elizabeth Brooks
Diplomat and Judge

Ellen Johnson Sirleaf
President

MADAGASCAR

Gisèle Rabesahala
Politician

MALAWI

Memory Banda
Teenage Activist

Joyce Banda
President

MALAYSIA

Che Siti Wan Kembang
Queen

Nicol David
Athlete

MALI

Aoua Kéita
Independence Activist

MEXICO

Comandanta Ramona
Indigenous Zapatista Leader

Concha Michel
Musician and Folklorist

Lydia Cacho
Journalist

Graciela Iturbide
Photographer

MONGOLIA

Khutulun
Athlete and Warrior

Mandukhai Khatun
Queen

MOROCCO

Fatema Mernissi
Sociologist

NEPAL

Puspa Basnet
Social Worker

Pasang Lhamu Sherpa
Mountaineer

NETHERLANDS

Frieda Belinfante
Conductor and Dutch
Resistance Member

Corrie ten Boom
Holocaust Rescuer

Aletta Henriëtte Jacobs
Inventor and Doctor

Judith Leyster
Painter

Hannie Schaft
Resistance Fighter

NEW ZEALAND

Jane Campion
Filmmaker

Dame Whina Cooper
Māori Leader

Parris Goebel
Hip-Hop Choreographer

NICARAGUA

Nora Astorga
Guerrilla Fighter and
U.N. Ambassador

NIGERIA

Amina Sukhera
Warrior

Margaret Ekpo
Women's Rights Activist
and Politician

Nana Asma'u
Princess and Poet

NORWAY

Katti Anker Møller
Reproductive Rights Advocate

Liv Ullmann
Film Director

PAKISTAN

Benazir Bhutto
Prime Minister

Begum Ra'ana Liaquat Ali Khan
Politician and Economist

Fatima Jinnah
Stateswoman and Dental Surgeon

PALESTINE

Fadwa Tuqan
Poet

Tarab Abdul Hadi
Feminist Activist

Wafaa Khater
Physicist

PERU

Flora Tristan
Feminist Writer

Micaela Bastidas Puyucahua
Independence Hero

Sofía Mulánovich
Surfer

Albina Ruiz Rios
Environmental Activist

PHILIPPINES

Corazon Aquino
President

Gabriela Silang
Freedom Fighter

Dr. Encarnacion A. Alzona
Historian

POLAND

Rosa Luxemburg
Politician

Wanda Rutkiewicz
Mountain Climber

Tamara Łempicka
Artist

Krystyna Krahelska
Poet

PORTUGAL

Isabella
Queen

Maria Isabel Barreno
Feminist Writer

PUERTO RICO

María Luisa Arcelay
Politician

Lolita Lebrón
Revolutionary

Carlota Matienzo Román
Teacher

ROMANIA

Nadia Comăneci
Gymnast

Herta Müller
Novelist

RUSSIA

Pussy Riot
Punk Band

Sofia Kovalevskaya
Mathematician

Anna Akhmatova
Poet

Valentina Tereshkova
Astronaut

SAUDI ARABIA

Haifaa al-Mansour
Filmmaker

Wajeha Al-Huwaider
Activist

SCOTLAND

Anna Munro
Suffragist

Elsie Inglis
Doctor

Victoria Drummond
Marine Engineer

SERBIA

Marina Abramović
Artist

SIERRA LEONE

Adelaide Casely-Hayford
Educator and Writer

SOMALIA

Hawa Aden Mohamed
Social Activist

Asha Haji Elmi
Politician

SOUTH AFRICA

Winnie Mandela
Activist and Politician

Lillian Masediba Ngoyi
Activist

Ellen Kuzwayo
Activist and Politician

SOUTH SUDAN

Margret Rumat Rumar Hassan
Olympic Runner

SPAIN

Teresa Perales Fernández
Olympic Athlete

Margarita Salas
Scientist

Lucía Sánchez Saornil
Anarchist Poet

Remedios Varo Uranga
Surrealist Painter

SRI LANKA

Sirimavo Ratwatte Dias Bandaranaike
Prime Minister

Mathangi "Maya" Arulpragasam (M.I.A.)
Singer and Activist

SUDAN

Emtithal Mahmoud
Poet

SWAZILAND

Patricia McFadden
Sociologist and Feminist

SWEDEN

Selma Lagerlöf
Author

Ellen Key
Writer

SWITZERLAND

Marie Goegg-Pouchoulin
Feminist Activist

SYRIA

Zenobia
Queen

Samar Yazbek
Journalist

THAILAND

Suriyothai
Queen

TIBET

Ani Pachen
Warrior Nun

TONGA

Sālote Tupou III
Queen

TRINIDAD AND TOBAGO

Claudia Jones
Activist and Journalist

TURKEY

Theodora
Empress

Fatma Aliye Topuz
Novelist

UNITED STATES

Queen Weetamoo
Native American Chief

Ida B. Wells
Journalist and Activist

Audre Lorde
Poet

Sylvia Rivera
Trans/Gay Rights Activist

URUGUAY

Delmira Agustini
Poet

UZBEKISTAN

Elena Urlaeva
Human Rights Activist

VENEZUELA

Luisa Cáceres de Arismendi
War Heroine

Teresa Carreño
Pianist, Singer, Composer, and Conductor

VIETNAM

The Trung Sisters
Military Leaders

Sister Chân Không
Peace Activist, and Spiritual Advisor

WALES

Sylvia Sleigh
Painter

YEMEN

Tawakkol Abdel-Salam Karman
Human Rights Activist and Journalist

Fatima al-Aqel
Disability Rights Activist

ZIMBABWE

Agnes Nyanhongo
Sculptor

Nehanda Charwe Nyakasikana
Spiritual Leader

ABOUT THE AUTHORS

Kate Schatz and Miriam Klein Stahl are the author and illustrator of *Rad American Women A-Z*. They live in the Bay Area and are both artists, educators, activists, and mothers.

A NOTE FROM THE WRITER

As I researched and wrote this book, during the summer and fall of 2015, the world often felt like a scary and sad place. News of war, terrorism, gun violence, and human suffering was relentless. Far away in lands distant from my own, people fled war, desperate to find new homes; here on the streets of America, police gunned down young black boys. Politicians and terrorists stoked hatred. Bullets flew, and tears fell.

It is no exaggeration to say that writing this book was a refuge for me. A reminder of the vast realities of historical suffering, and the enormous capacity for love and change. Every day I sought solace in the stories of these women whose lives were tragic and triumphant, inspiring and encouraging. When the forces of evil seemed to dominate the events of the world, these accounts reminded me that women have overcome, fought back, led, created, invented, achieved, and succeeded. We have climbed mountains, planted trees, crossed continents. We have protected land and language. We have always been there. And always will be.

There's a famous saying that "history is written by the victors." I agree, but I'd also say that history is written by the writers—and I am one. And that's why I've made you this book.

A NOTE ON THE ART

The papercut illustrations in this book were created by Miriam Klein Stahl, using paper, pencil, and an X-Acto knife.

A NOTE ON THE RESEARCH

In this book we have done our best to be thorough and thoughtful with our research. Whenever possible we used primary sources, and always consulted a vast range of secondary and tertiary sources. Even though the stories are relatively short, we read *a lot* about each woman! We used books, and we used the Internet. We watched interviews and documentaries, and we listened to songs and albums. We consulted experts and locals, young people and elders, historians and feminists. Because we are based in the United States, and thus have a limited range of worldwide knowledge, we reached out to people from countries all over the world to get input and feedback on these stories. Many of the living women reviewed and approved their stories, and family members, scholars, and other trusted individuals reviewed many of the additional stories. We are so grateful to those people who read each story carefully to ensure cultural, regional, and historical accuracy.

Throughout history, the stories of many legendary figures have been turned into just that—legends. It becomes hard to determine what is fact and what is fiction, especially when researching people who lived long, long ago, whose stories have been told and retold many times. It's especially common for the life stories of women to become sensationalized; these accounts often include details intended to shock, surprise, or even scandalize. And to make stories extra-interesting, accuracy is often sacrificed as tales get retold. We've made every effort to present true, well-researched stories of real-life rad women.

ACKNOWLEDGMENTS

This book has been made possible by the support, love, input, wisdom, and generosity of many individuals from all over the world.

Thank you so much to our families: Jason, Ivy, and Benson Pontius; Lena Wolff and Hazel Klein Wolff; Barbara and Doug Schatz; Nancy Murray; Aubrey Schatz; Judi Bertolin; Judith and Julian Stahl; Daniela Sea; Lisa and Patrick Higgins; Robert and Jen Stahl

To our agents: Charlotte Sheedy and Steven Malk

To the Ten Speed team: Julie Bennett, Clara Sankey, Emma Campion, and Angelina Cheney

To City Lights Books: Elaine Katzenberger, Stacey Lewis, and Chris Carosi

And to the following rad individuals for their support, wisdom, input, childcare, ideas, opinions, and love:

Niambi Allah
Chiara Barzini
Lisa Brown
Tammy Rae Carland
Chloe Charlton
Masami Chin
Aaron Cometbus
Todd Elkin
Marcus Ewert
Sarah Sophie Flicker
Teri Goodman
Jen Hofer
Kate Hurowitz
Julia Mayer
Nikki McClure
Sachi Moran
Ace Morgan
Innosanto Nagara
Catherine Newman
Prof. Marcia Ochoa
Casey and Boff Orr
Carolyn Pennypacker-Riggs
Micah Perks
Sadia Rahman
Lea Redmond
Lucy Rosenthal
Jos Sances
Will Schwartz
JayT Scott
Amy Sonnie
Anna Joy Springer
Ruby Sullivan
Mariko Tamaki
Michelle Tea
Rachel Thieme
Leslie Van Every
Maria van Lieshout
Gabe & Terri

. . . and everyone else who has weighed in and offered support online and in person

The following people provided invaluable feedback and edits to each story in the book:

Chloe Ashley
Anne Atwood
Brooke Bocast
Tisa Bryant
Javier Cabra
Puawai Cairns
Anne Chambers
Rae Chang
Tom Cho
Winifred Conkling
Dr. Kara Cooney
Heidi Cregge
Carolina DeRobertis
Cathy Dewes
Dr. Candace Falk
Olive Fontaine
Birutė Mary Galdikas
Molly Gardner
Liza Gesuden
Lauren Gucick
Cami Hall
Stephanie Hanis
Dr. Maria Jaschok
Cynthia Jordan
Keiran King
Kathy Kleiman
Jackie Ko
Dr. Khin Mar Mar Kyi
Jennifer Lash
Wanjira Maathai
John Mataira
Katerina Mataira
Ratu Mataira
Mia McDonald
Dr. Larissa Mercado-Lopez
Hindatu Mohammed
Kirthi Nath
Chinaku Onyemelukwe
Siv Parker
Jenn Phillips
Martin Rowe
Buffy Sainte-Marie
Lisa Sorenson
Ella Zalon